11+ Non-Verbal Reasoning
For GL Assessment

It's no secret that the GL 11+ test can be seriously tricky. But don't worry — this CGP Practice Book will give children a brilliant headstart on their test preparation.

In the first few sections, they can practise answering questions on one concept at a time. Then, when they're ready for more realistic 11+ practice, give the Assessment Tests a try.

It's all set at just the right level for Ages 8-9, so it's perfect for building their confidence. And with detailed answers included at the back of the book, marking is a breeze!

How to access your free Online Edition

This book includes a free Online Edition to read on your PC, Mac or tablet. You'll just need to go to cgpbooks.co.uk/extras and enter this code:

1588 0361 7034 4801

By the way, this code only works for one person. If somebody else has used this book before you, they might have already claimed the Online Edition.

Practice Book — Ages 8-9
with Assessment Tests

How to use this Practice Book

This book is divided into three parts — Spotting Patterns, Spatial Reasoning* and Assessment Tests. There are also answers and detailed explanations at the back of the book.

*Not all GL Assessment Non-Verbal Reasoning tests will include Spatial Reasoning questions — it depends on the region in which your child is sitting the test. If you are in a region that does not test Spatial Reasoning, then you can ignore the questions on p.14-19, as well as Assessment Test 11 (p.80-85).
For more information on test content in different regions, please visit cgpbooks.co.uk/11plus.

Spotting Patterns

- Each section contains practice questions focusing on one of the main concepts your child will need to understand for the Non-Verbal Reasoning test.
- These pages can help your child build up the different skills they'll need for the real test.
- Your child can use the smiley face tick boxes in this section and in the Spatial Reasoning section to evaluate how confident they feel with each topic.

Spatial Reasoning

- This part concentrates on the skills your child will need to tackle the Spatial Reasoning questions that are tested in some regions.

Assessment tests

- The third part of the book contains eleven assessment tests, each with a mix of question types. They take a similar form to the real test.
- You can print multiple-choice answer sheets so your child can practise the tests as if they're sitting the real thing — visit cgpbooks.co.uk/11plus/answer-sheets or scan the QR code.

- Use the printable answer sheets if you want your child to do each test more than once.
- If you want to give your child timed practice, give them a time limit of 15 minutes for each test, and ask them to work as quickly and carefully as they can.
- Tests 1-10 get progressively harder, so don't be surprised if your child finds the later ones more tricky.
- Your child should aim for a mark of around 85% (24 questions correct) in each test. If they score less than this, use their results to work out the areas they need more practice on.
- If they haven't managed to finish the test in time, they need to work on increasing their speed, whereas if they have made a lot of mistakes, they need to work more carefully.
- Keep track of your child's scores using the progress chart at the back of the book.

Published by CGP
Editors:
Ceara Hayden, Sharon Keeley-Holden, Anthony Muller and Rebecca Tate

With thanks to Claire Boulter and Alexandra Reynolds for the proofreading.
Please note that CGP is not associated with GL Assessment in any way. This book does not include any official questions and is not endorsed by GL Assessment.

ISBN: 978 1 78908 161 9
Printed by Zenith Print & Packaging Ltd, Pontypridd.
Clipart from Corel®

Based on the classic CGP style created by Richard Parsons
Text, design, layout and original illustrations © Coordination Group Publications Ltd. (CGP) 2018
All rights reserved.

Photocopying this book is not permitted, even if you have a CLA licence.
Extra copies are available from CGP with next day delivery • 0800 1712 712 • www.cgpbooks.co.uk

Contents

Tick off the check box for each topic as you go along.

Spotting Patterns

Shapes .... 2 ✓
Counting 4
Pointing 6
Shading and Line Types 7
Order and Position.. 8
Rotation 10
Reflection 11
Layering 12

Spatial Reasoning

3D Shapes 14
Folding 16
Hidden Shape 18
Connecting Shapes 19

Assessment Tests

Test 1 20
Test 2 26
Test 3 32
Test 4 38
Test 5 44
Test 6 50
Test 7 56
Test 8 62
Test 9 68
Test 10 74
Test 11 80

Glossary 86
Answers 87
Progress Chart 102

Spotting Patterns

Shapes

Looking at the shapes in a question is often a good place to start.

Warm Up

1. How many **sides** does each shape have?

   a.  b.  c.  d.  e.  f.

   5 ___ ___ ___ ___ ___ ___

2. How many of the **grey shapes** on the right have the **same number** of **sides** as the grey shape inside the square?

   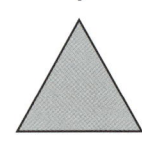 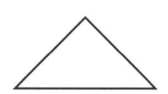  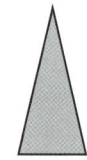  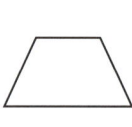

   Number of **same-sided** grey shapes: ____

Find the Figure Like the First Two

Work out which of the figures on the right is most like the two figures on the left.

Example:

 |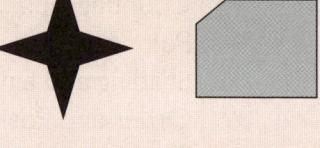

                           a   b   c   d   e

All figures must have three sides. (**b**)

3.   |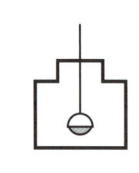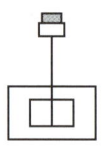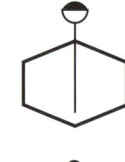

                           a   b   c   d   e

(____)

4. 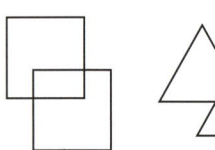 |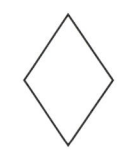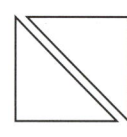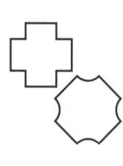

                           a   b   c   d   e

(____)

5. 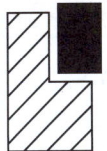  |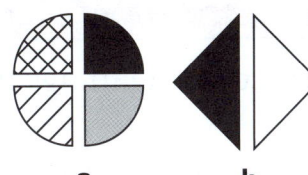

                                      a   b   c   d   e

(____)

Vertical Code

Each question has three figures on the left with code letters that describe them. You need to work out what the code letters mean. The figure on the right is missing its code. Work out which of the five codes describes this figure.

Example:

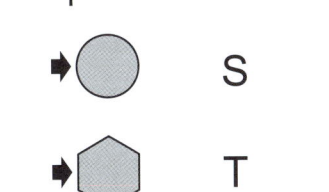

                        T   Q   R   S   P

                        a   b   c   d   e

S means a grey circle. T means a grey hexagon. (a)

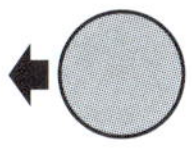

6.  X

 Z   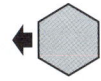   W   Z   Y   V   X

 Y   a   b   c   d   e

(____)

7. FL

 GM   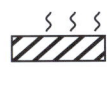 GM   FL   FM   LM   GL

                       a   b   c   d   e

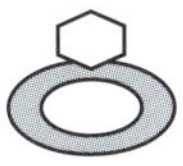

 FM

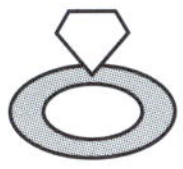

(____)

8.  CP

 BQ    BP   CQ   CP   DQ   DP

                      a   b   c   d   e

 DP

(____)

Spotting Patterns

Counting

A lot of questions can be solved by counting things like shapes or dots.

Warm Up

1. How many **circles** are there in each figure?

   a. 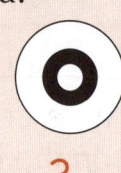 b.  c. 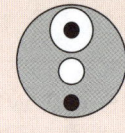 d. 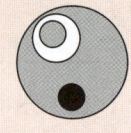 e.  f.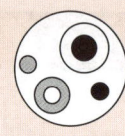

   <u>3</u>   ___   ___   ___   ___   ___

2. How many of these cakes have the **same** number of **layers** as the one inside the square? How many have the **same** number of **cherries**?

   Number of cakes with the **same number** of **layers**: ___

   Number of cakes with the **same number** of **cherries**: ___

Complete the Series

The squares on the left are arranged in order. One of the squares is empty. Work out which of the squares on the right should replace the empty square.

Example:

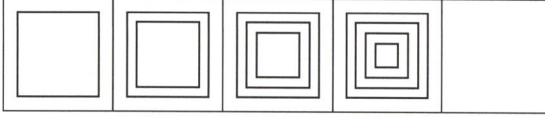    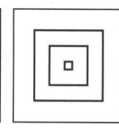 

a   b   c   d   e

An extra square is added in each series square. (<u>b</u>)

3.

a   b   c   d   e

(___)

4.

a   b   c   d   e

(___)

5.

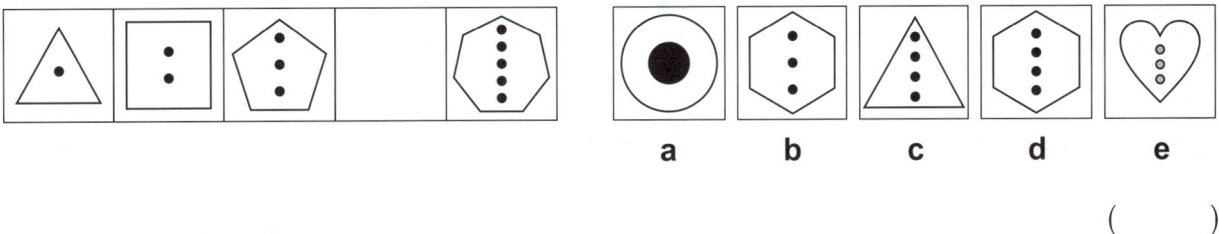

( )

Find the Figure Like the First Three

Find the figure on the right that is most like the three figures on the left.
Example:

All figures must have two inner shapes that are identical to the outer shape apart from size and shading.   (b)

6.

   |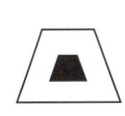
                                                  a   b   c   d   e

( )

7.

   |

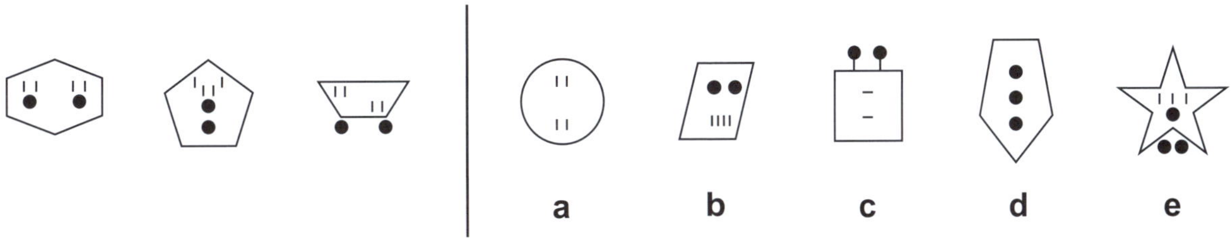

                                                  a   b   c   d   e

( )

8.

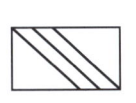   |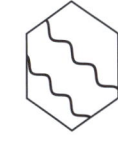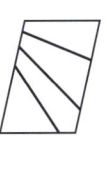

                                                  a   b   c   d   e

( )

Spotting Patterns

Pointing

The direction that an arrow points in is just as important as what it is pointing at.

Warm Up

1. What **shape** is the **white arrow** pointing at?

   a.  b.  c.  d.  e.  f.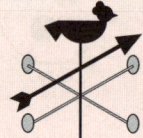

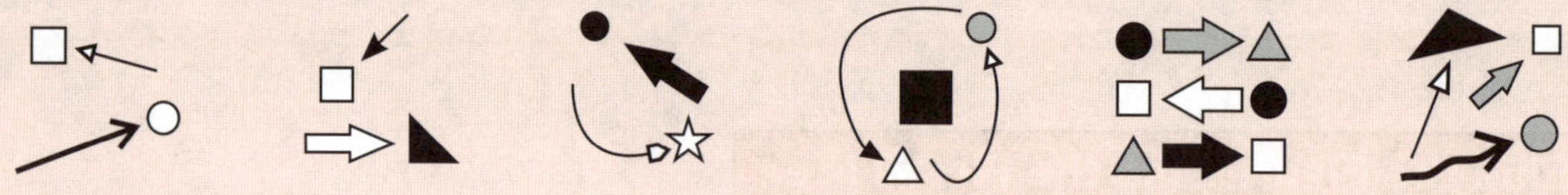

   square _____ _____ _____ _____ _____

2. How many of the **arrows** on the right point in the **same direction** as the arrow in the square?

   Arrows can also point in a clockwise or anticlockwise direction (see p.86).

   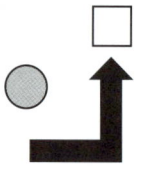 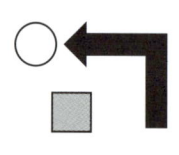 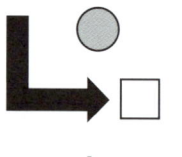 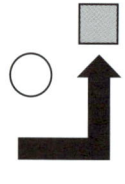

   Number of **arrows** that point in the **same direction**: ____

Odd One Out

Look at the five figures below. Find the figure that is most unlike the others.
Example:

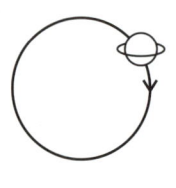 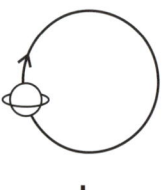  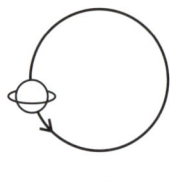 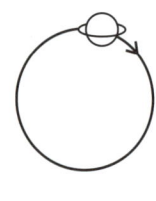

   a   b   c   d   e

In all other figures, the arrow points towards a square. In C it points towards a circle. (**C**)

3.

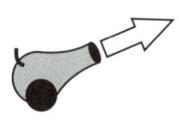 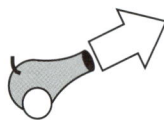   

   a   b   c   d   e

(____)

4.

   a   b   c   d   e

(____)

Spotting Patterns

Shading and Line Types

Shading is how a shape is coloured and line type is how its lines are drawn.

Warm Up

1. What **colour** are **most** of the shapes in each figure?

   a. 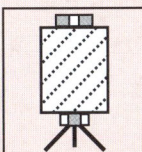   b. 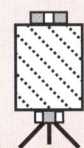   c. 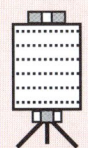   d. 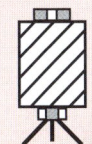   e. 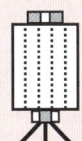   f.

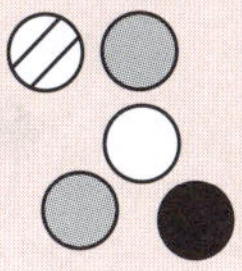

   grey _____ _____ _____ _____ _____

2. How many paintings have the **same direction** of **hatching** as the painting in the square? How many have the **same type** of **line** (dotted or solid)?

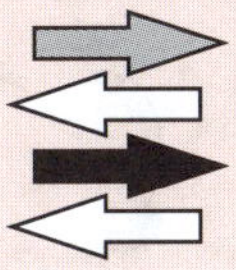

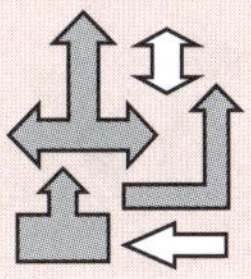

   Number of paintings with the **same direction** of **hatching**: ____

   Number of paintings with the **same type** of **line**: ____

Odd One Out

Look at the five figures below. Find the figure that is most unlike the others.
Example:

  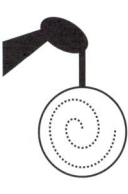  

a   b   c   d   e

In all other figures, the big shape has a dashed outline. In D it has a dotted outline. (d)

3.

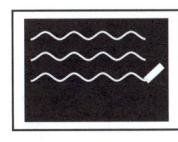 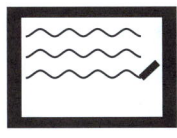 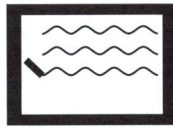  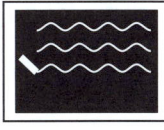

a   b   c   d   e

(____)

4.

a   b   c   d   e

(____)

Spotting Patterns

Order and Position

Shapes can be in different positions inside a figure. They can also change order.

Warm Up

1. Which shape is **one place clockwise** from the **circle** in each figure?

   a. 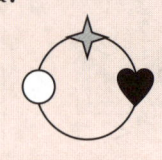 b. 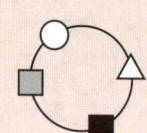 c.  d.  e.

   star   _____   _____   _____   _____

2. How many figures on the right have the **same order** of **shapes** going from top to bottom as the figure inside the square (ignoring size)?

   Number of figures with the **same order** of **shapes**: ____

Find the Figure Like the First Three

Work out which of the figures on the right is most like the three figures on the left.

Example:

   |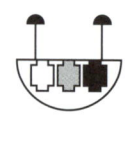

　　　　　　　　　　　　　　　　　a　　　b　　　c　　　d　　　e

In all figures, the three inner shapes go from left to right in the order: black, grey, white. (_e_)

3.    |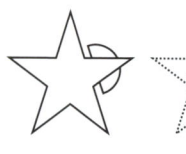

　　　　　　　　　　　　　　　　　　a　　　b　　　c　　　d　　　e

(____)

4. 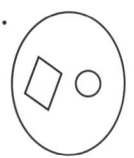 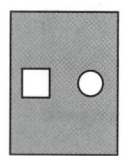  |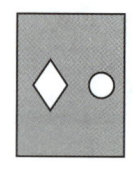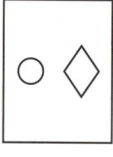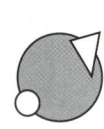

　　　　　　　　　　　　　　　　　　a　　　b　　　c　　　d　　　e

(____)

Spotting Patterns

5.

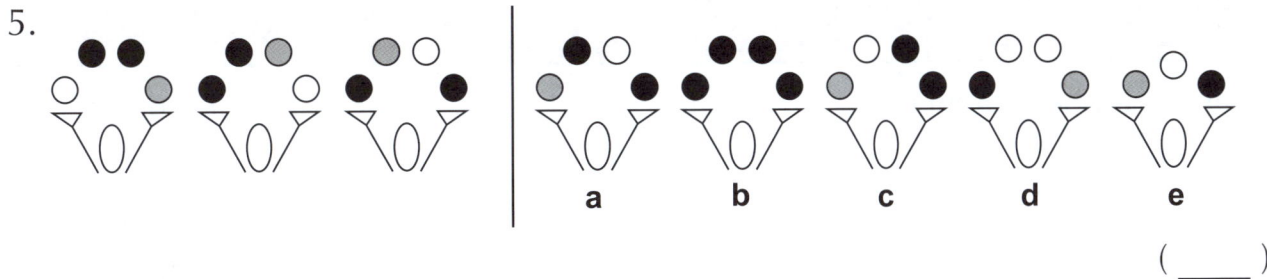

(____)

Complete the Pair

The first figure in each question changes to become the second figure. Work out how the first figure has been changed. Then find the figure on the right that would match the third figure if it was changed in the same way.

Example:

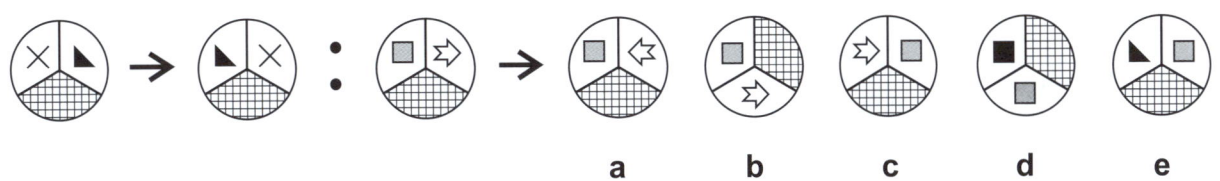

The top left hand shape and the top right hand shape swap places. (C)

6.

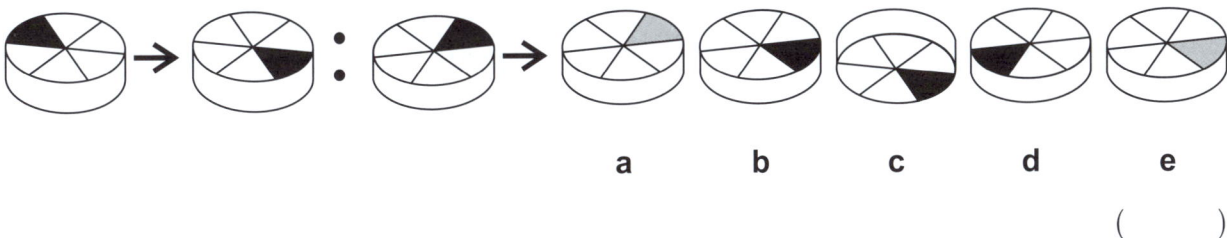

(____)

7.

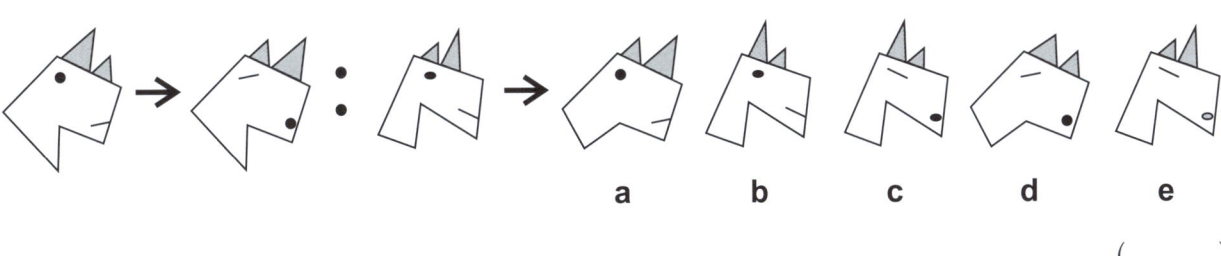

(____)

8.

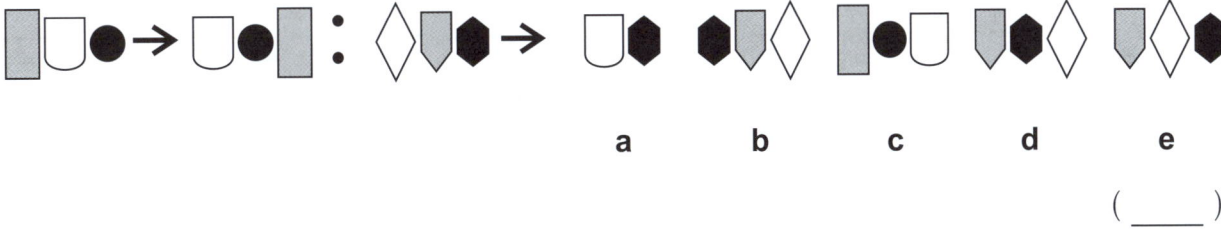

(____)

Spotting Patterns

Rotation

Shapes can be rotated (turned) by different amounts, and in two different directions.

Warm Up

1. The **black** shapes are rotated **90 degrees** to become the **white** shapes. Work out if they are rotated clockwise (**C**) or anticlockwise (**A**).

   a.    b.    c.    d.    e.    f.

   _C_   ___   ___   ___   ___   ___

2. How many figures on the right are **identical** to the figure inside the square apart from being **rotated differently**?

   See p.86 for more about rotation.

   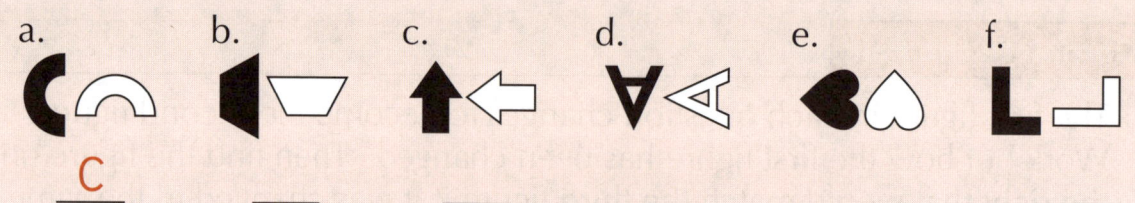

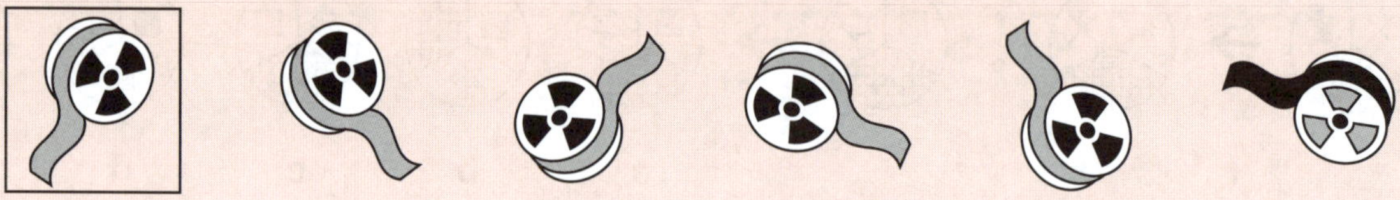

   Number of **identical figures**: ___

Complete the Series

The squares on the left are arranged in order. One of the squares is empty. Work out which of the squares on the right should replace the empty square.

Example:

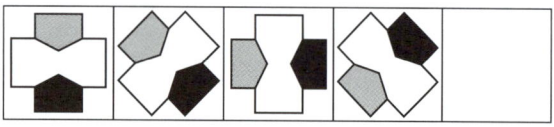   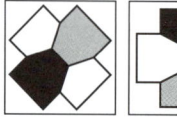 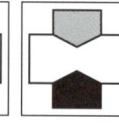 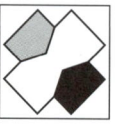 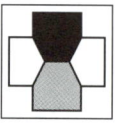
                                                      a   **b**   **c**   **d**   **e**

The figure rotates 45 degrees anticlockwise in each series square. (_b_)

3.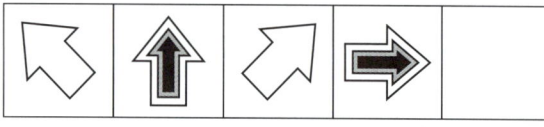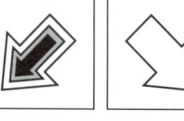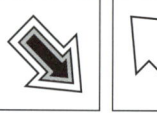

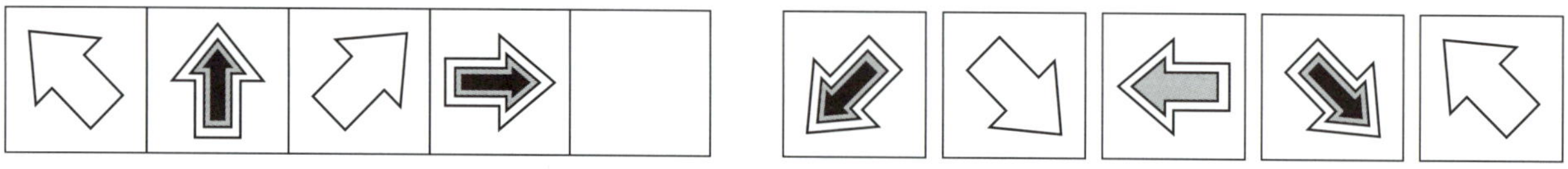

                                          a   **b**   **c**   **d**   **e**

(___)

4.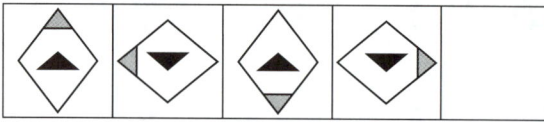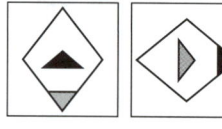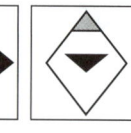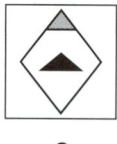

                                          a   **b**   **c**   **d**   **e**

(___)

Spotting Patterns

Reflection

The reflection of a shape is how it would look in a mirror.

Warm Up

1. Is the black shape a **sideways reflection** of the white shape?

   a. b.  c. d.  e.  f.

     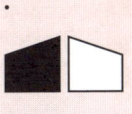

   yes ____ ____ ____ ____ ____

2. How many of these figures are **reflections** of the figure inside the square?

   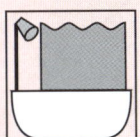 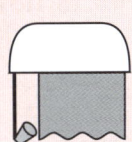 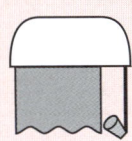 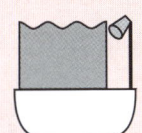 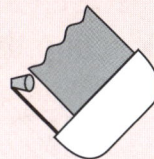 

   Number of **reflections**: ____

Complete the Pair

The first figure in each question changes to become the second figure. Work out how the first figure has been changed. Then find the figure on the right that would match the third figure if it was changed in the same way.

Example:

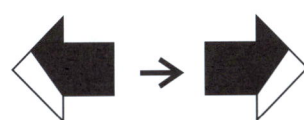 :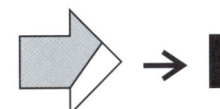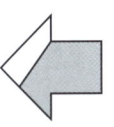

                                  a   b   c   d   e

The figure reflects across. (_e_)

3.  :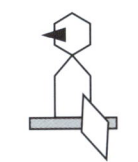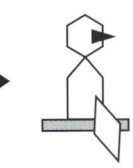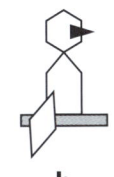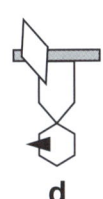

                                  a   b   c   d   e

(____)

4. 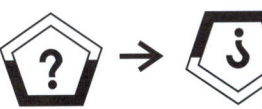 :

                                  a   b   c   d   e

(____)

Spotting Patterns

Layering

Shapes are layered if they overlap each other.

Warm Up

1. What **shape** is at the **front** of each of the figures below?

   a. 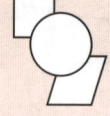 b.  c.  d. 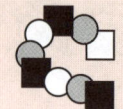 e.  f.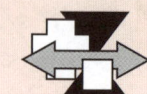

   circle _____ _____ _____ _____ _____

2. How many ice creams have a **front scoop** that is **hatched**, and a **back scoop** that is **grey**?

   Number of ice creams: ____

Odd One Out

Look at the five figures below. Find the figure that is most unlike the others.
Example:

  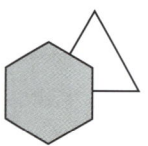 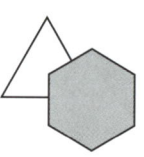 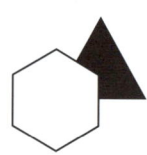

　a　　　　　　　b　　　　　　　c　　　　　　　d　　　　　　　e

In all other figures, the hexagon is in front of the triangle. (b)

3.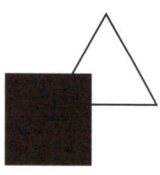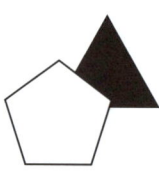

　a　　　　　　　b 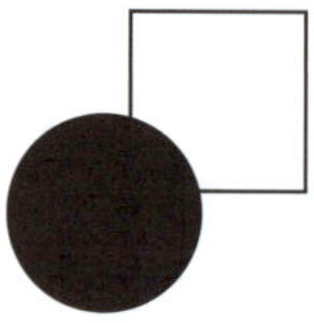　　　　　　　c　　　　　　　d　　　　　　　e

(____)

4.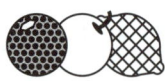

　a　　　　　　　b　　　　　　　c　　　　　　　d　　　　　　　e

(____)

Spotting Patterns

5.

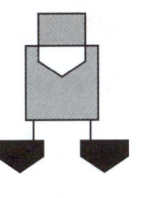  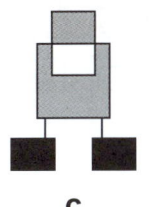 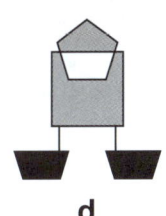 

a b c d e

(____)

Complete the Pair

The first figure in each question changes to become the second figure. Work out how the first figure has been changed. Then find the figure on the right that would match the third figure if it was changed in the same way.

Example:

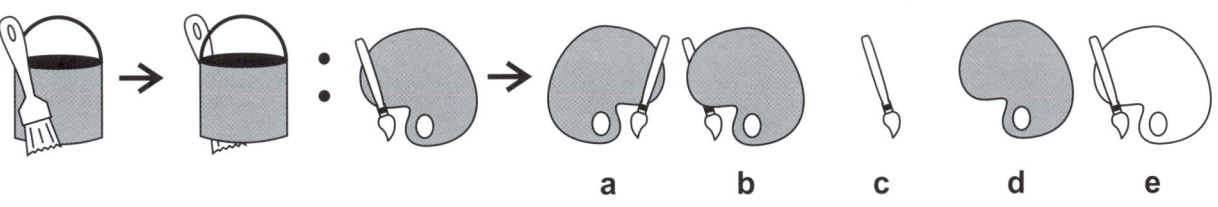

a b c d e

The shape at the front moves to the back. (b)

6.

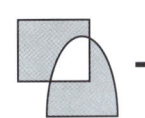   

a b c d e

(____)

7.

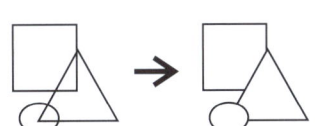  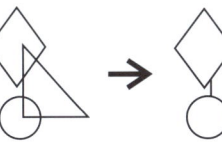 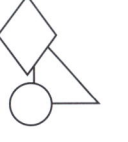 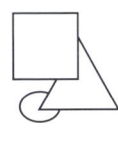  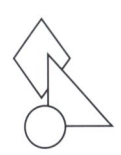 

a b c d e

(____)

8.

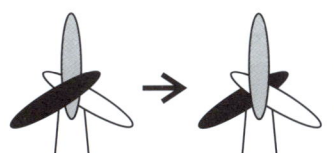 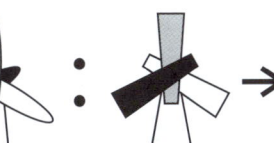 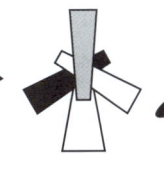   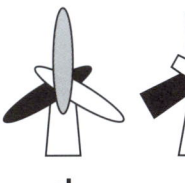 

a b c d e

(____)

Spotting Patterns

, # Spatial Reasoning

3D Shapes

You might need to imagine what a 3D shape would look like from different angles.

Warm Up

1. If you looked at each figure from **above**, how many cubes could you see?

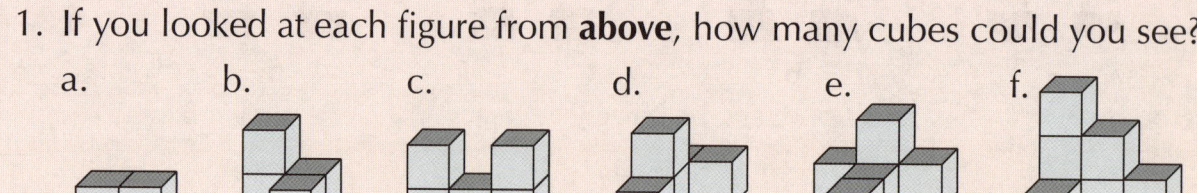

   a. 2   b. ___   c. ___   d. ___   e. ___   f. ___

2. How many of these figures are **different** views of the figure in the square?

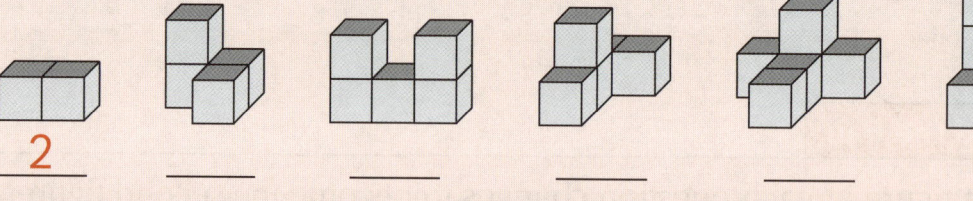

Number of figures: ___

Look at the Figure from the Top

Look at the figure on the left. What would it look like if you saw it from the top? Choose the option on the right which looks like this.

Example:

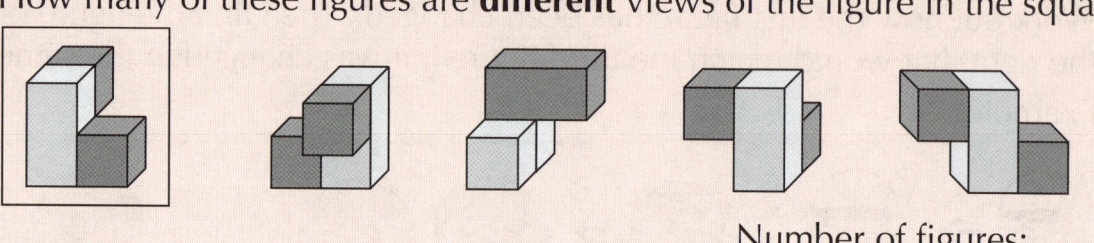

  a   b   c   d   e

Four cubes are visible from the top and there is one cube at the front of the figure. (c)

3.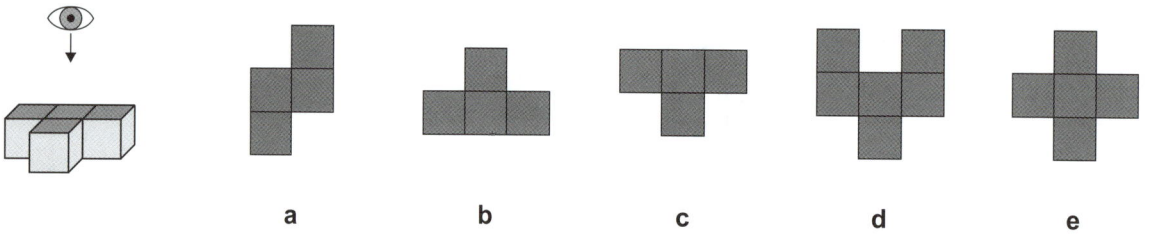

   a   b   c   d   e

   (___)

4.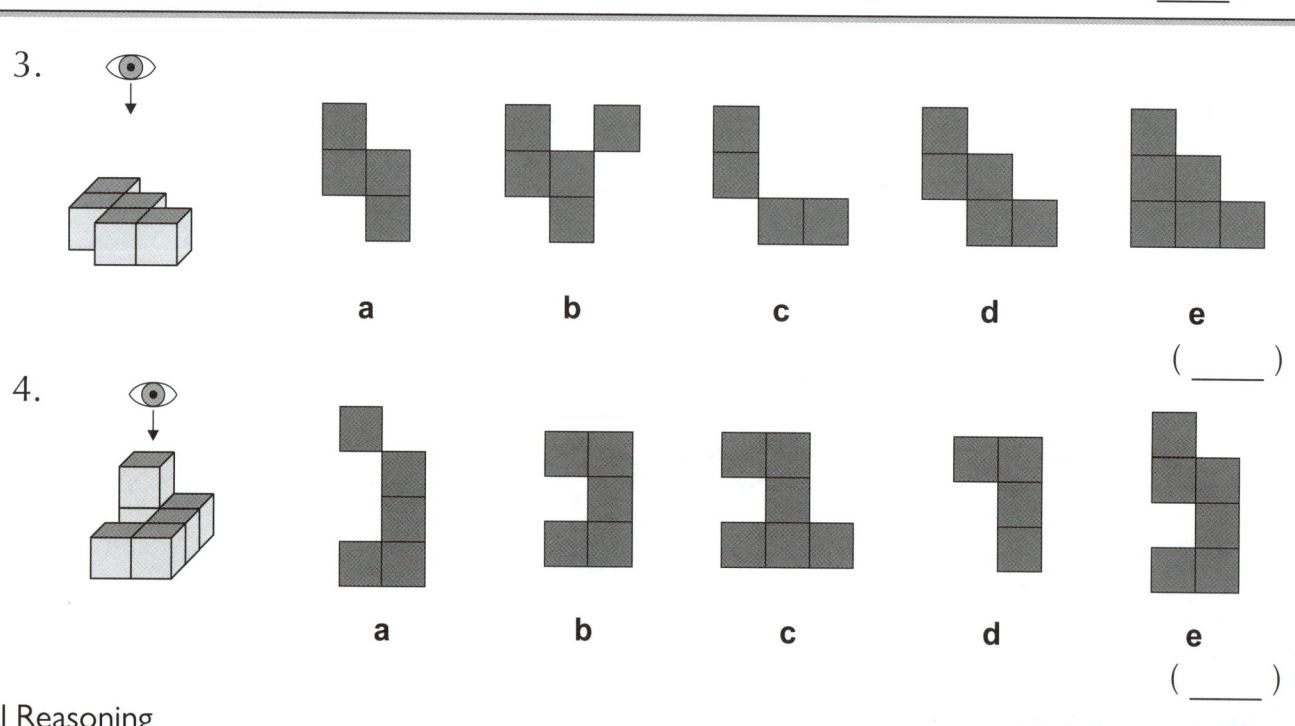

   a   b   c   d   e

   (___)

5.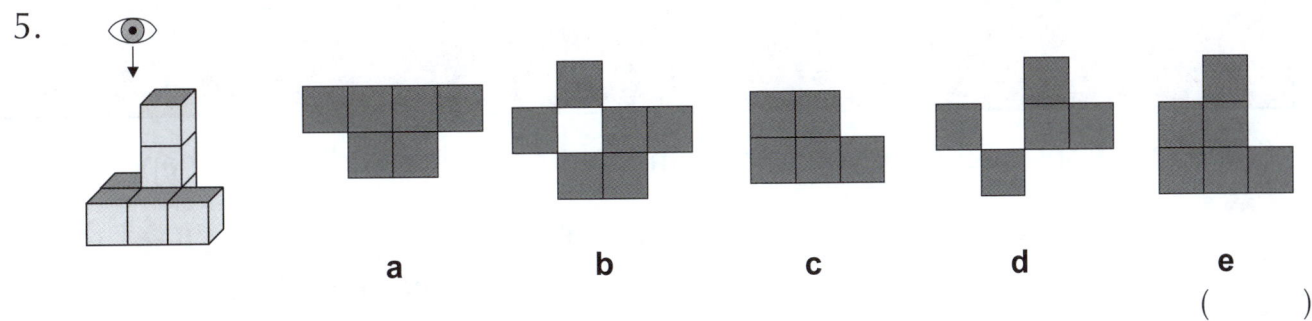

(___)

Look at the Figure from the Right

Look at the figure on the left. What would it look like if you saw it from the right-hand side? Choose the option on the right which looks like this.

Example:

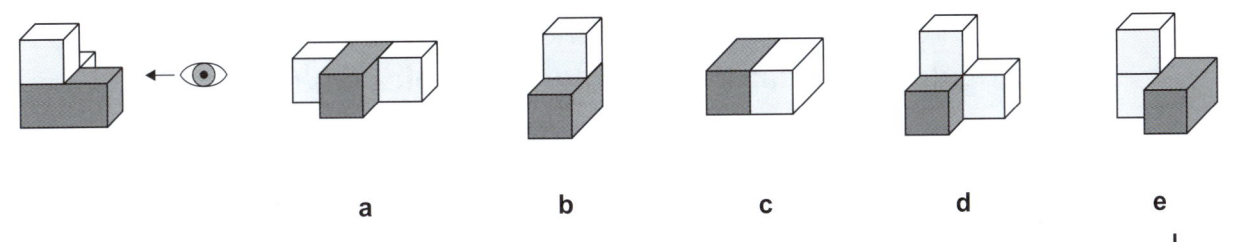

There is a long grey block with one white cube on top and another on the right-hand side. (d)

6.

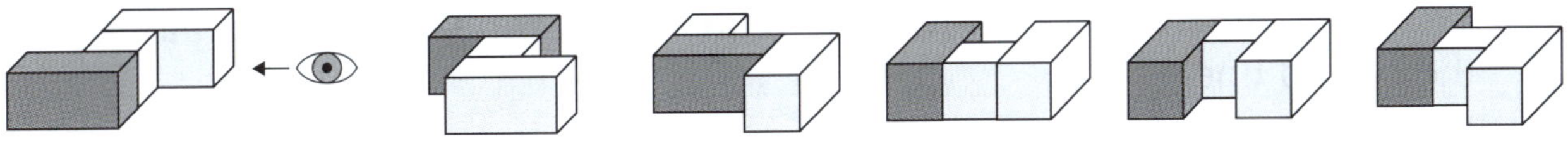

a b c d e

(___)

7.

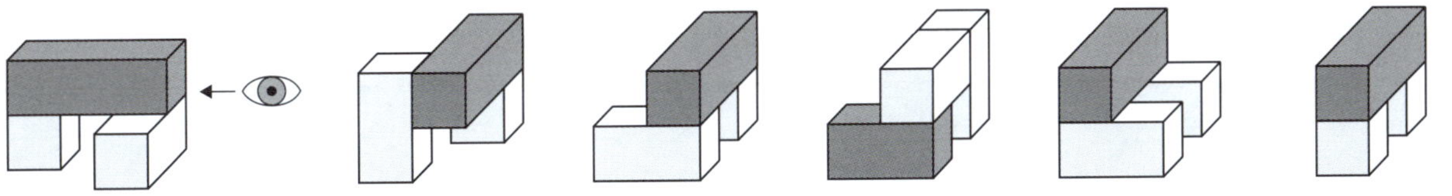

a b c d e

(___)

8.

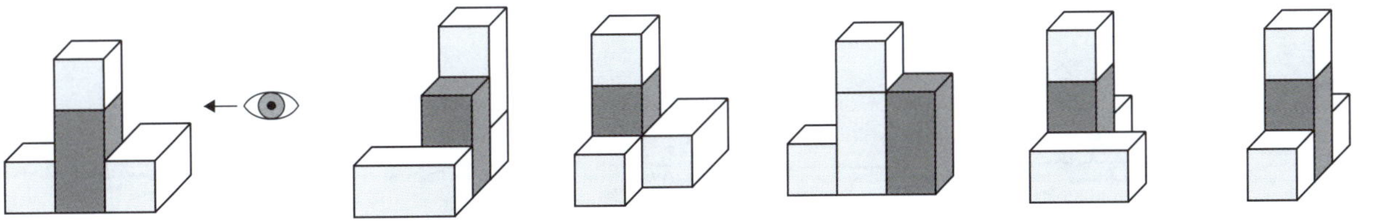

a b c d e

(___)

Spatial Reasoning

Folding

Some questions might ask you to imagine folding and unfolding 2D shapes.

Warm Up

1. Imagine that the shape on the left is **folded** along the **dotted line**. Does the figure on the right correctly show the **folded shape**? Write **yes** or **no**.

   a. 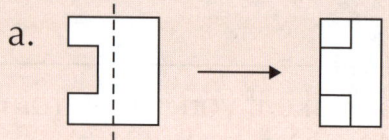   b.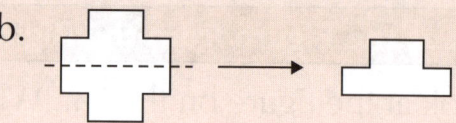

   _____   _____

2. The square on the left is **folded** in half and then a circle is **punched** through it. Imagine that the square is then **unfolded**. On the right hand square, draw where the **holes** would be.

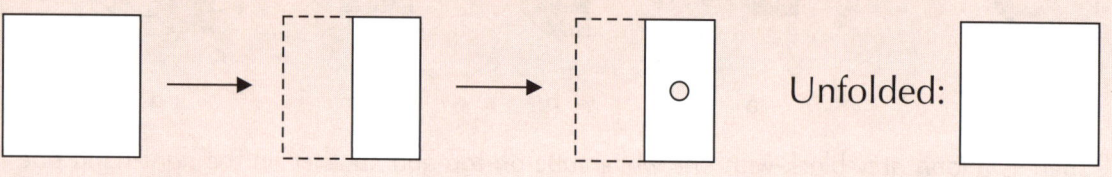

Fold Along the Line

Work out which option shows the figure on the left when folded along the dotted line.

Example:

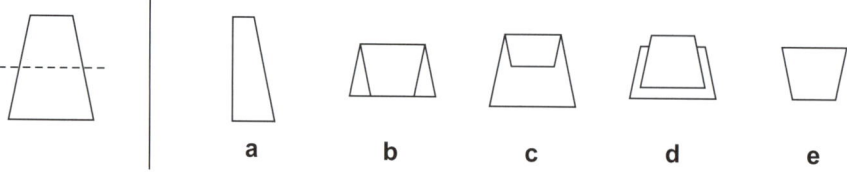

(**b**)

In options A and C, the fold line has moved. Option D has been broken apart along the fold line. In option E, the part of the figure originally below the fold line should still be visible.

3.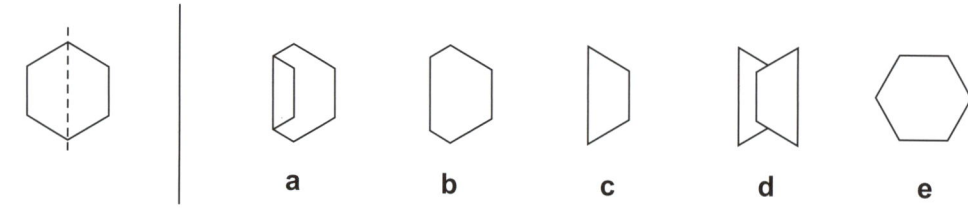

(___)

4.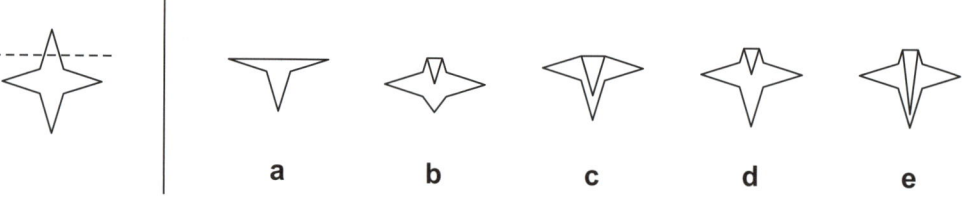

(___)

Spatial Reasoning

5.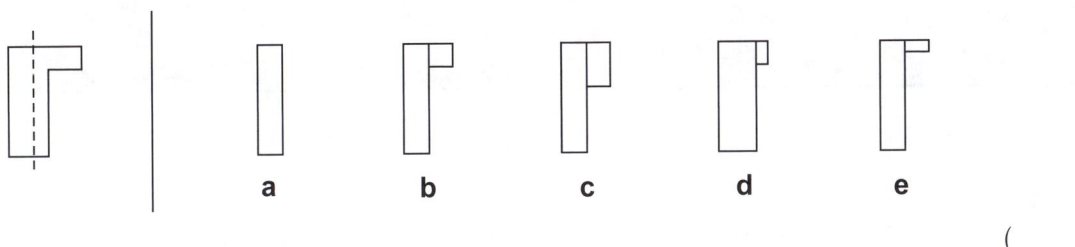

(___)

Fold and Punch

A square is folded and then a hole is punched, as shown on the left. Work out which option shows the square when unfolded.

Example:

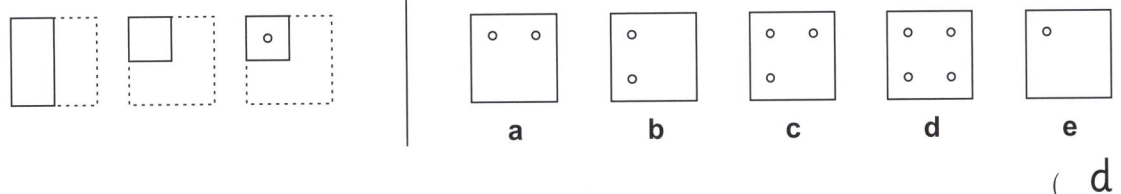

(d)

6.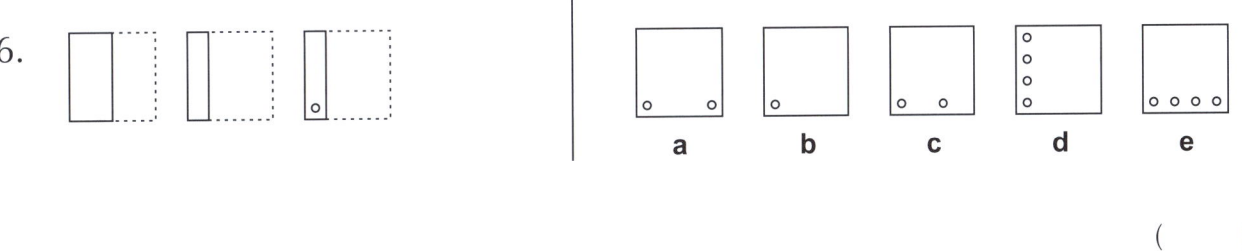

(___)

7.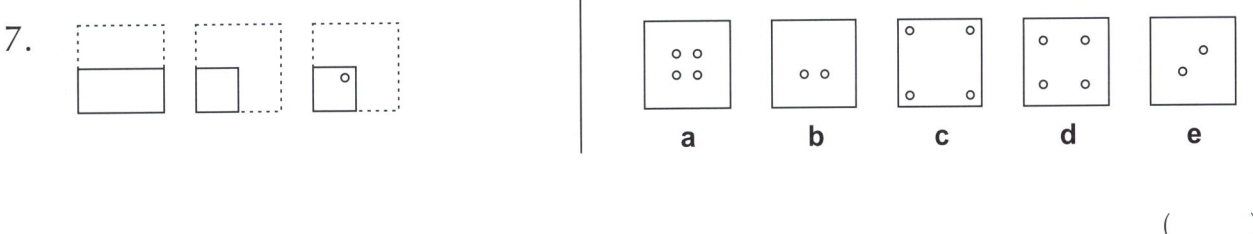

(___)

8.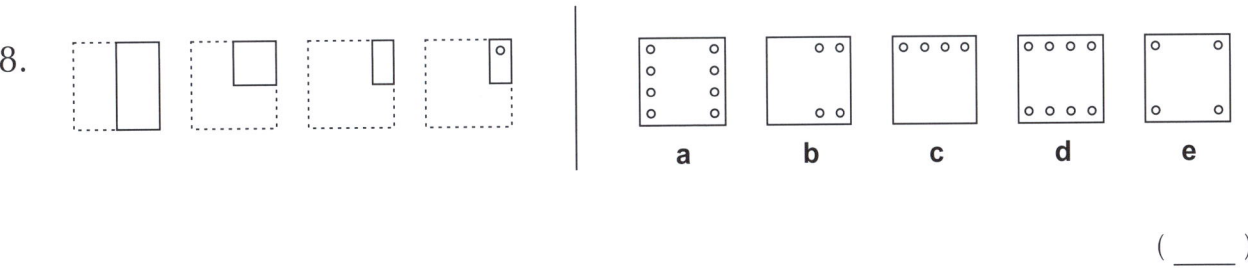

(___)

Spatial Reasoning

Hidden Shape

You might get questions asking you to find a hidden shape.

Warm Up

1. Which shape (a to e) is **identical** to the triangle in the figure on the left?

    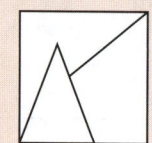   a.   b.   c.   d.   e.

    Shape: ____

2. Shade in the **square** in each of the figures below.

    a. 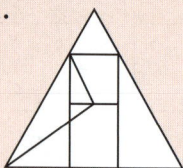   b. 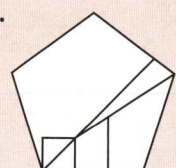   c.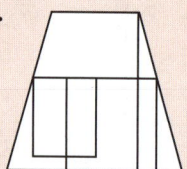

Hidden Shape

Work out which option contains the hidden shape shown.
It should be the same size and orientation.
Example:

 |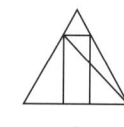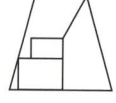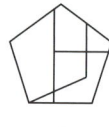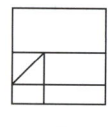
　　　　　　　　　　a　　　　b　　　　c　　　　d　　　　e   (_d_)

The hidden shape is here: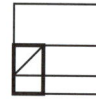

3. |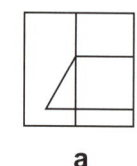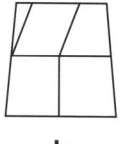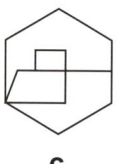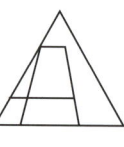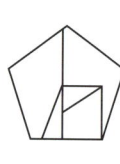
　　　　　　　　　　a　　　　b　　　　c　　　　d　　　　e

(___)

4. |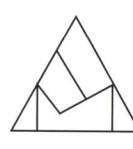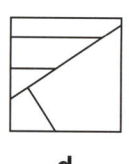
　　　　　　　　　　a　　　　b　　　　c　　　　d　　　　e

(___)

Spatial Reasoning

Connecting Shapes

You might need to imagine what some shapes will look like when joined together.

Warm Up

1. The **letters** show the **sides** where the two shapes should be joined together. Which figure shows the shapes joined **correctly**?

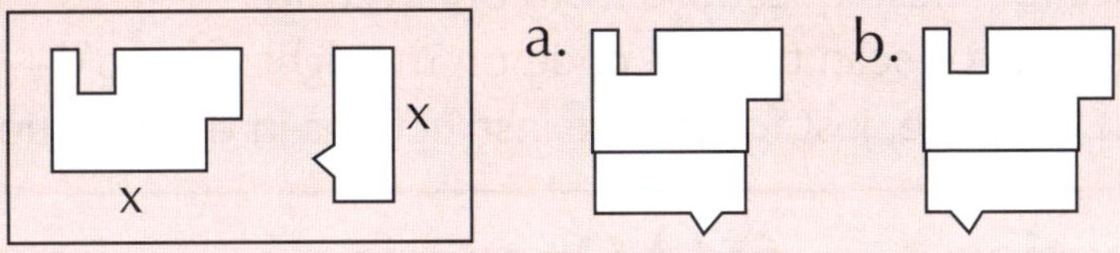

   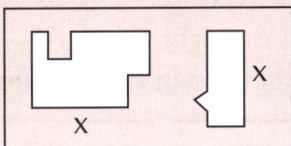 a. 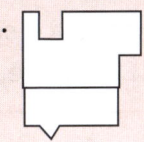 b.

   Figure: _____

2. In the box on the right, **draw** a picture to show the shapes joined by the **correct** sides.

   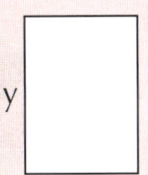 

Connecting Shapes

Work out which option shows how the three shapes will look when they are joined by matching the sides with the same letter.

Example:

(C)

Options A, D and E are ruled out because both rectangles are connected to the wrong sides of the trapezium. Option B is ruled out because the wrong side of the small rectangle is connected to the trapezium.

3. 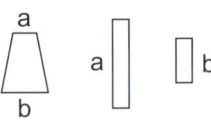 |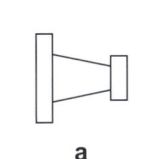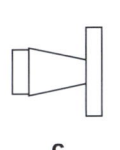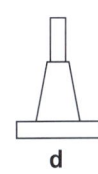
                                 a   b   c   d   e

   (____)

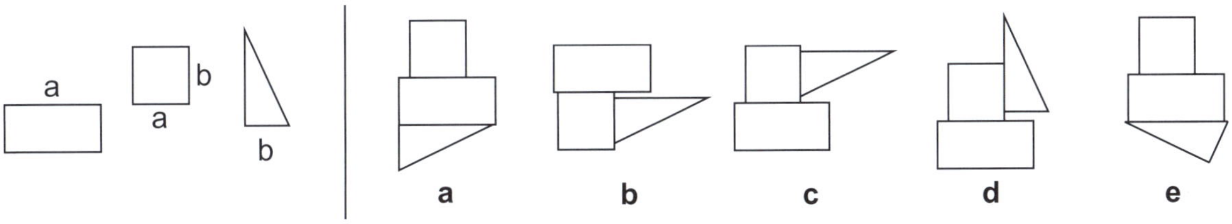

4. 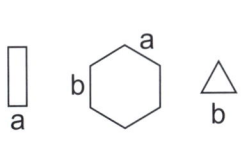 |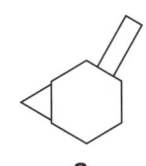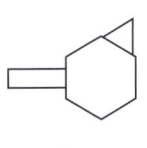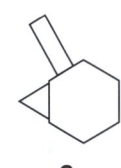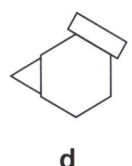
                                 a   b   c   d   e

   (____)

Spatial Reasoning

Assessment Test 1

This book contains eleven assessment tests, which get harder as you work through them to help you improve your NVR skills.

Allow around 15 minutes to do each test and work as quickly and as carefully as you can.

If you want to attempt each test more than once, you will need to print **multiple-choice answer sheets** for these questions from our website — go to cgpbooks.co.uk/11plus/answer-sheets or scan the QR code on the right. If you'd prefer to answer the questions on the page, just follow the instructions in the question.

Section 1 — Odd One Out

Each of the questions below has five figures.
Find the figure in each row that is most unlike the others.

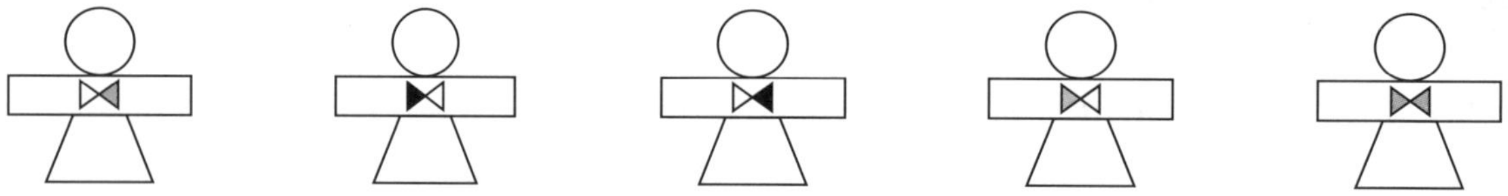

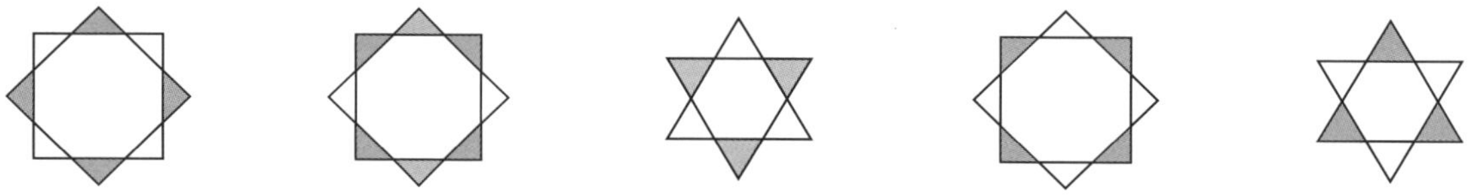

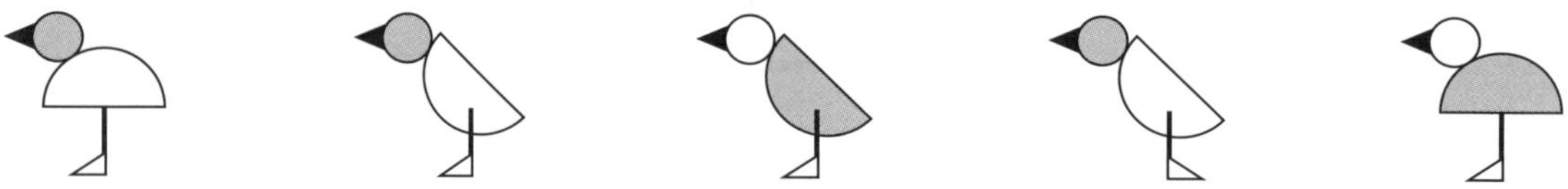

Example:

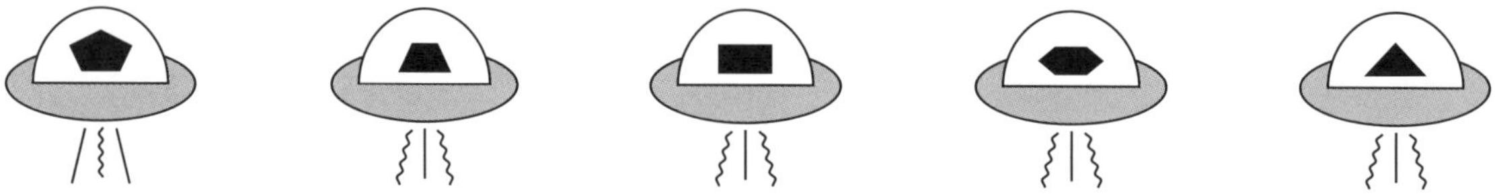

Answer: b

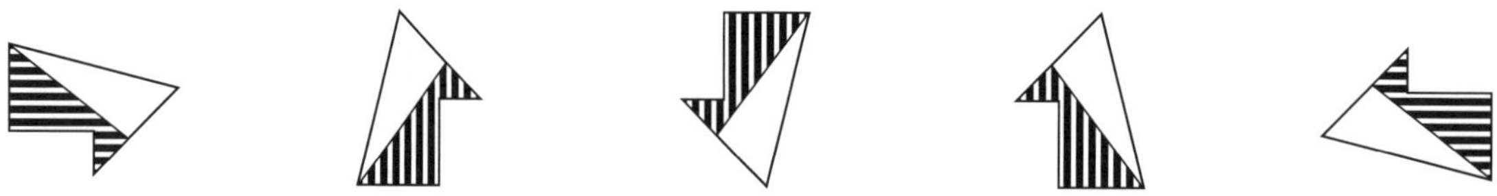

Section 2 — Complete the Pair

The first figure in each question changes to become the second figure. Work out how the first figure has been changed. Then find the figure on the right that would match the third figure if it was changed in the same way.

Example:

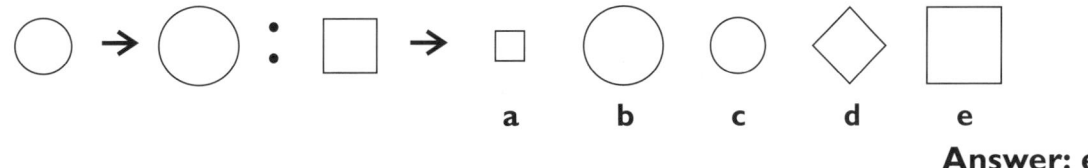

Answer: e

(1)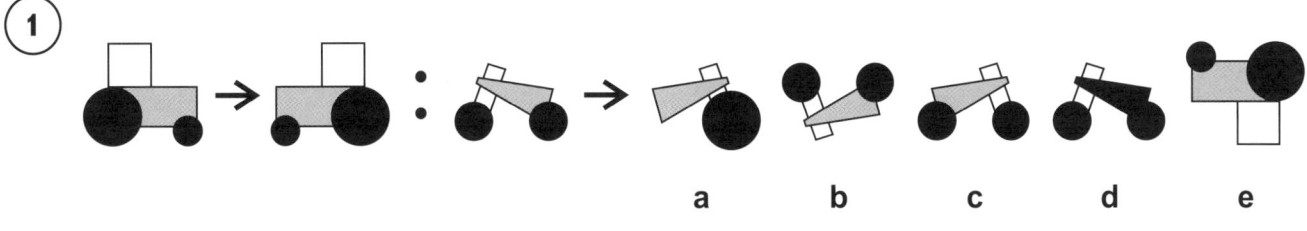

(2)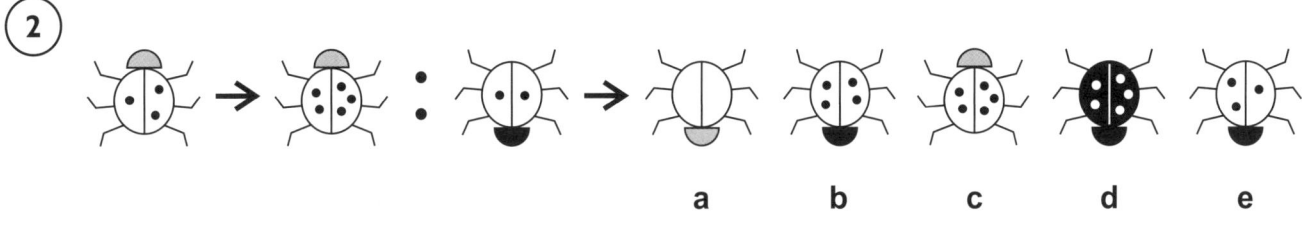

(3)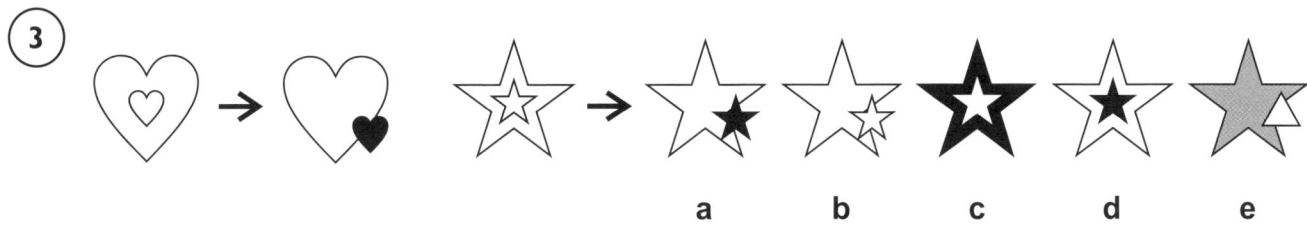

(4)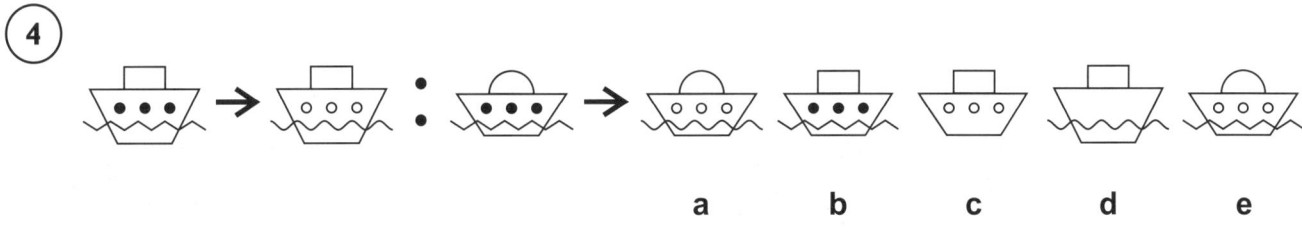

(5)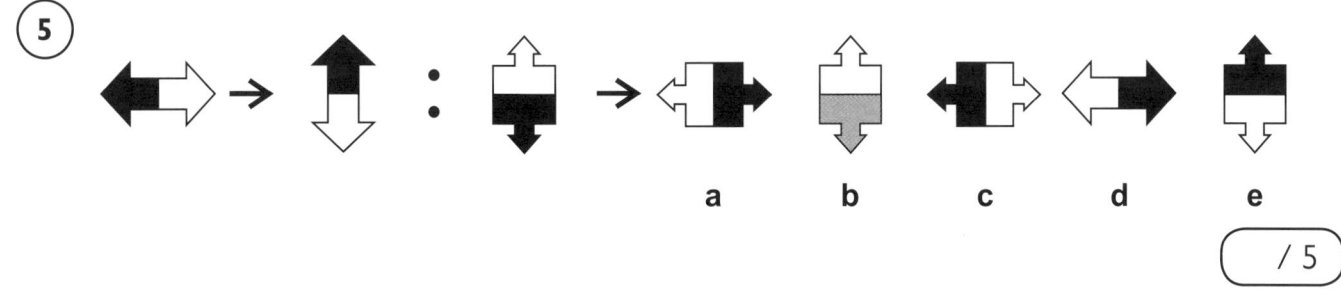

/ 5

Carry on to the next question → →

Assessment Test 1

Section 3 — Complete the Grid

On the left of each question below is a grid with one empty square.
Work out which of the five squares on the right should replace the empty square.

Example:

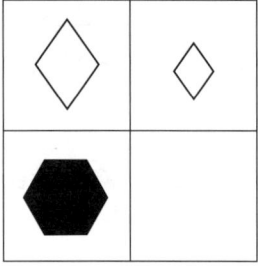      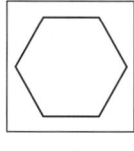 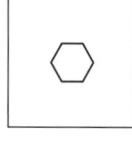

                                           a   b   c   d   e

Answer: c

1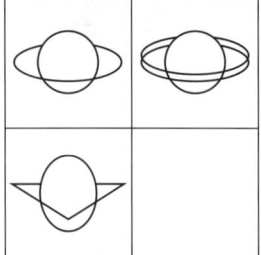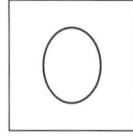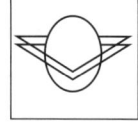

                                          a   b   c   d   e

2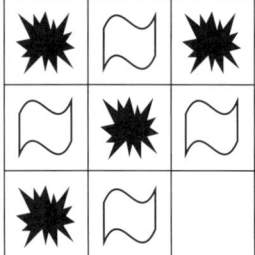

                                          a   b   c   d   e

3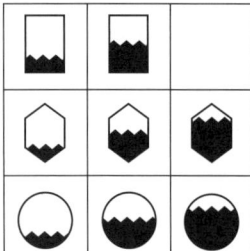

                                          a   b   c   d   e

4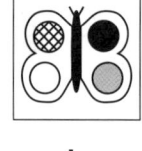

                                          a   b   c   d   e

/ 4

Assessment Test 1

Section 4 — Find the Figure Like the First Two

In each question, there are two figures on the left that are like each other in some way. Work out which of the five figures on the right is most like the two figures on the left.

Example:

  |

a   b   c   d   e

Answer: c

(1) 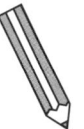  |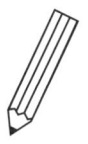

a   b   c   d   e

(2)  |

a   b   c   d   e

(3) 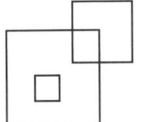 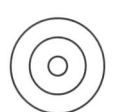 |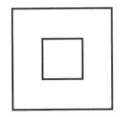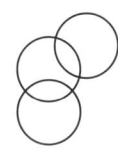

a   b   c   d   e

(4)   |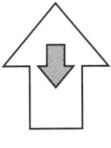

a   b   c   d   e

(5) 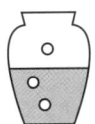 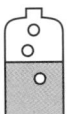 |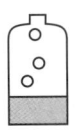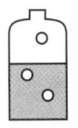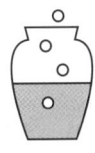

a   b   c   d   e

Carry on to the next question → →

Assessment Test 1

Section 5 — Complete the Series

Each of these questions has five squares on the left that are arranged in order. One of the squares is empty. Work out which of the five squares on the right should replace the empty square.

Example: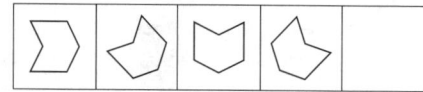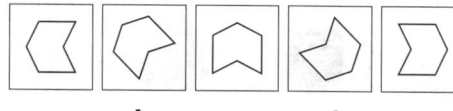

Answer: a

1.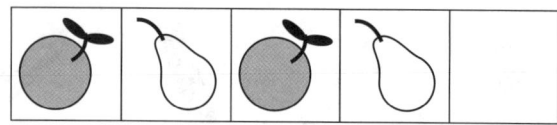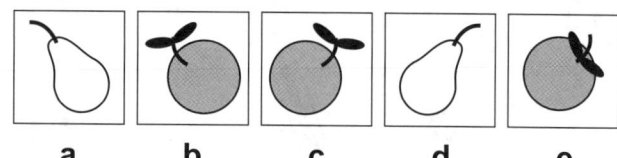

2.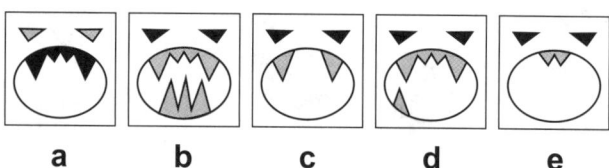

3.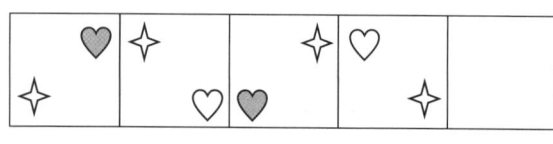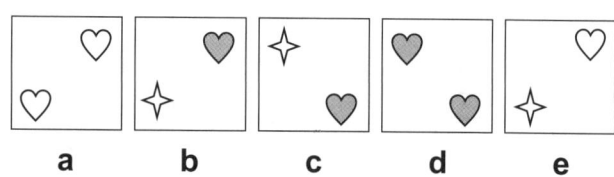

4.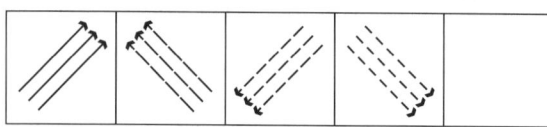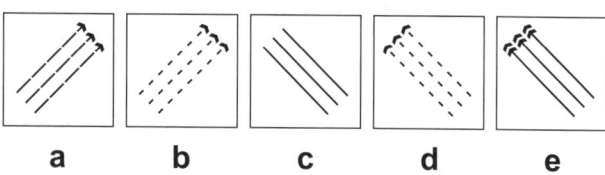

5.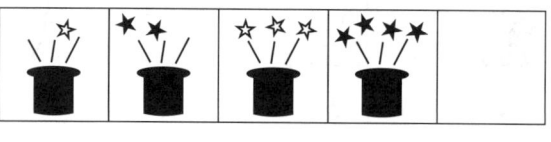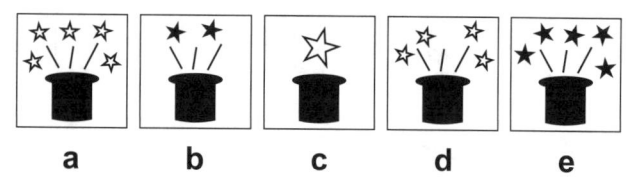

/ 5

Assessment Test 1

Section 6 — Vertical Code

Each question has three figures on the left with code letters that describe them. You need to work out what the code letters mean. The figure on the right is missing its code. Work out which of the five codes on the right describes this figure.

Example:  P

⇧ Q

⇦ R

 P   Q   T   S   R
       a   b   c   d   e

Answer: a

The arrow pointing right has the code letter P. The arrow pointing up has the code letter Q. The arrow pointing left has the code letter R. The figure on the right is an arrow pointing right, so its code must be P and the answer is **a**.

---

1   X

   Y

   Y

   Z   X   W   Y   V
   a   b   c   d   e

---

2   KM

   LM

   KN

   KM   KN   LK   LN   LM
   a   b   c   d   e

---

3   FP

   GP

   GQ

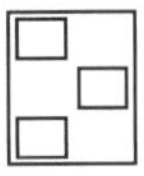

   GQ   FQ   GP   FG   FP
   a   b   c   d   e

---

4   JS

    KT

    JT

     JT   JS   LS   KS   KT
         a   b   c   d   e

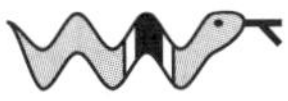

/ 4   Total   / 28

End of Test

Assessment Test 1

Assessment Test 2

You can print **multiple-choice answer sheets** for these questions from our website — go to cgpbooks.co.uk/11plus/answer-sheets or scan the QR code on the right. If you'd prefer to answer them in standard write-in format, just circle the letter underneath your answer. The test should take around 15 minutes.

Section 1 — Complete the Pair

The first figure in each question changes to become the second figure. Work out how the first figure has been changed. Then find the figure on the right that would match the third figure if it was changed in the same way.

Example:

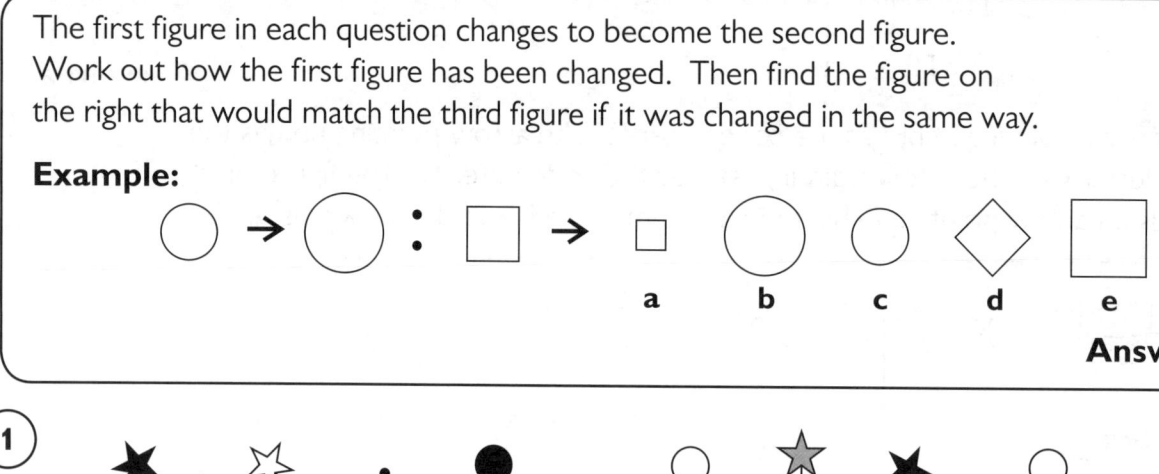

Answer: e

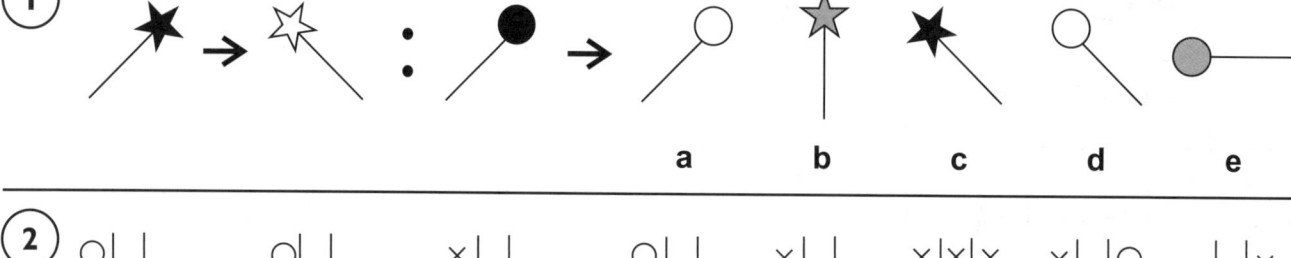

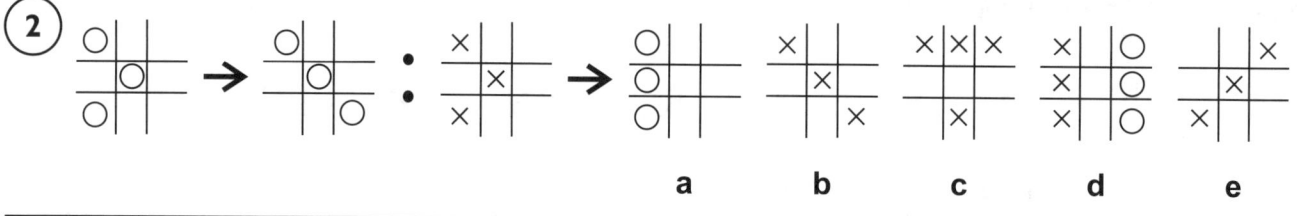

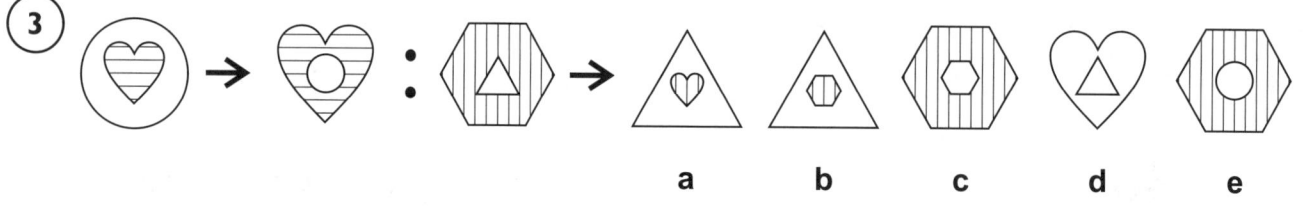

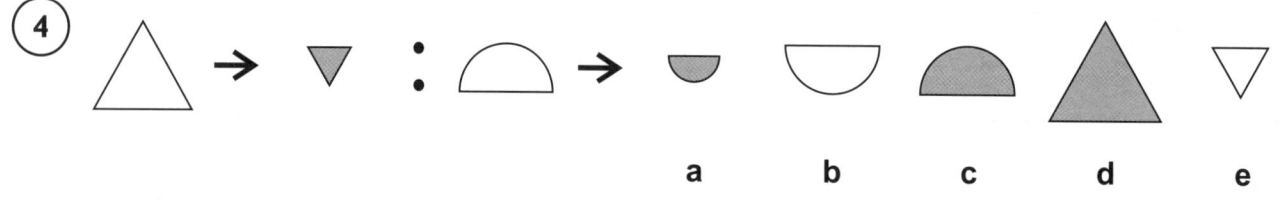

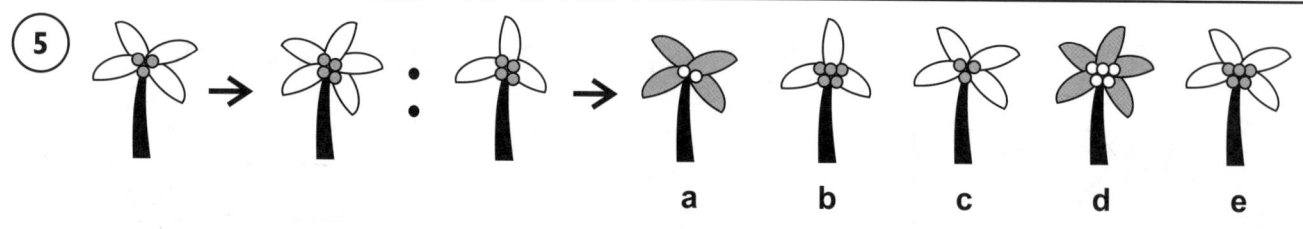

/ 5

Section 2 — Complete the Series

Each of these questions has five squares on the left that are arranged in order. One of the squares is empty. Work out which of the five squares on the right should replace the empty square.

Example: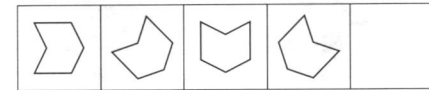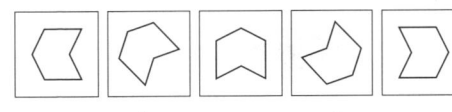

Answer: a

(1)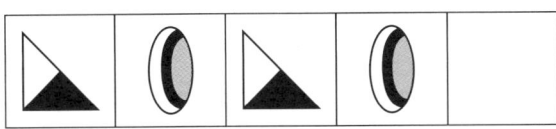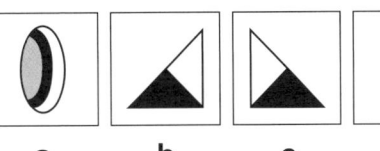

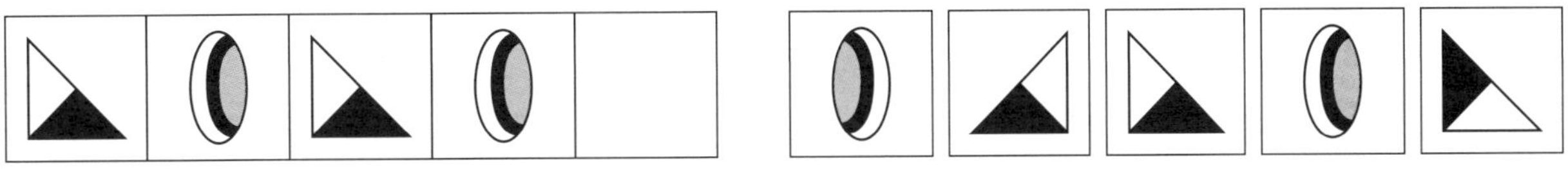

(2)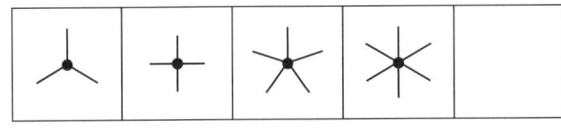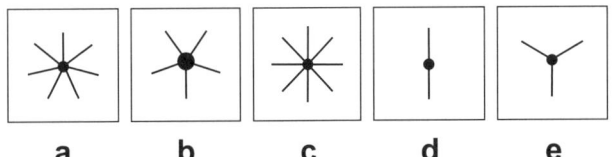

(3)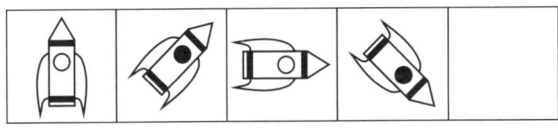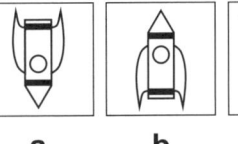

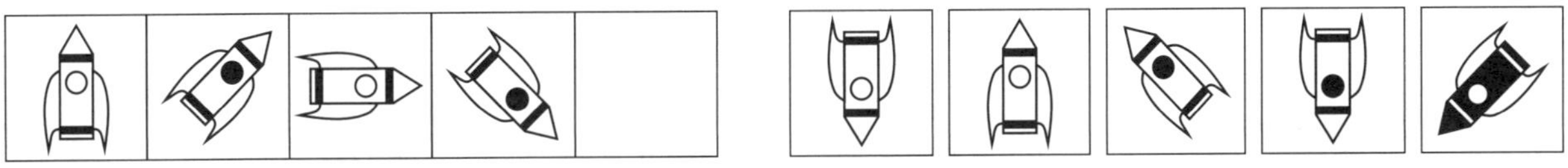

(4)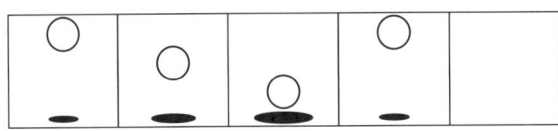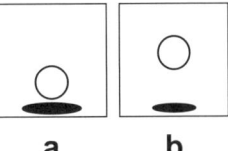

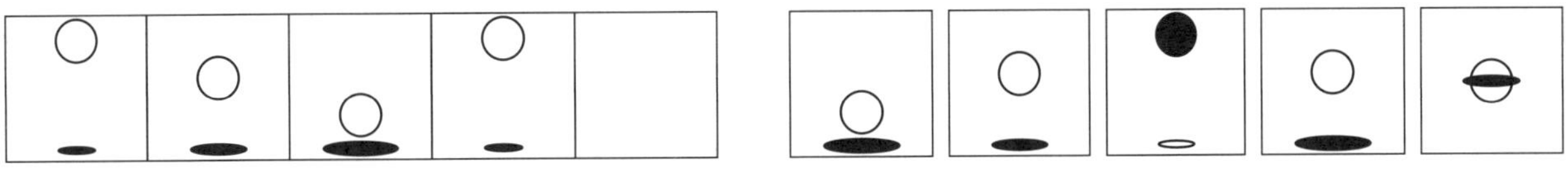

(5)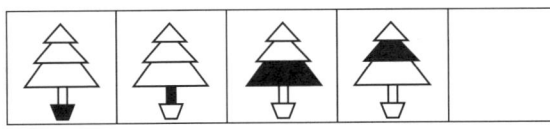

/ 5

Carry on to the next question → →

Assessment Test 2

Section 3 — Odd One Out

Each of the questions below has five figures.
Find the figure in each row that is most unlike the others.

Example:

a b c d e

Answer: b

(1)

a b c d e

(2)
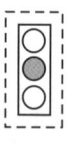  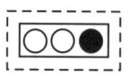  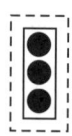

a b c d e

(3)

a b c d e

(4)
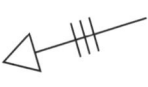    

a b c d e

(5)
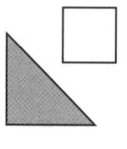 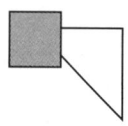 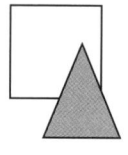 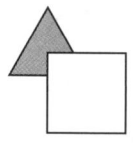 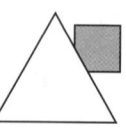

a b c d e

/ 5

Assessment Test 2

Section 4 — Vertical Code

Each question has three figures on the left with code letters that describe them. You need to work out what the code letters mean. The figure on the right is missing its code. Work out which of the five codes on the right describes this figure.

Example:

⇨	P					
⇧	Q	⇨	P	Q	T	S	R
⇦	R		a	b	c	d	e

Answer: a

The arrow pointing right has the code letter P. The arrow pointing up has the code letter Q. The arrow pointing left has the code letter R. The figure on the right is an arrow pointing right, so its code must be P and the answer is **a**.

---

1  M

 L   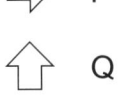   P   L   N   M   R
               a   b   c   d   e

 M

---

2 XZ

 YZ   □   YZ   YW   YX   XY   XW
                   a   b   c   d   e

 XW

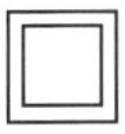

---

3  AP

 CQ   BQ   CP   BP   AB   AQ
                   a   b   c   d   e

 BP

---

4 ES

 GT   EG   EF   GS   FT   ET
                   a   b   c   d   e

 FS

/ 4

Carry on to the next question → →

Assessment Test 2

Section 5 — Complete the Grid

On the left of each question below is a grid with one empty square.
Work out which of the five squares on the right should replace the empty square.

Example:

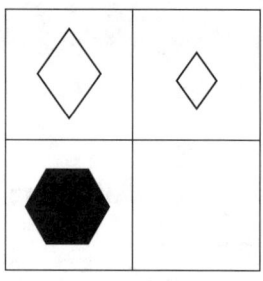 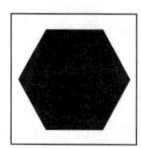   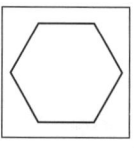 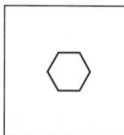

a b c d e

Answer: c

1

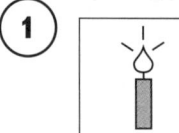     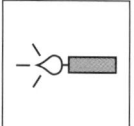

a b c d e

2

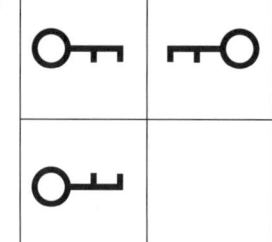     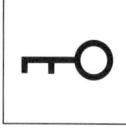

a b c d e

3

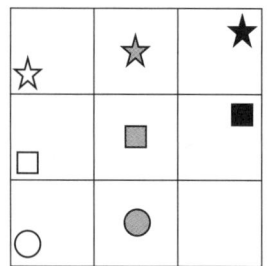 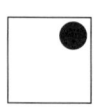  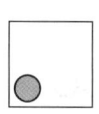

a b c d e

4

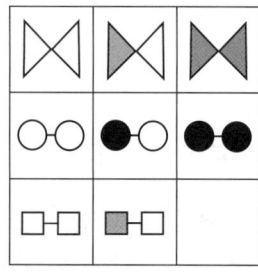  

a b c d e

/ 4

Assessment Test 2

Section 6 — Find the Figure Like the First Three

In each question, there are three figures on the left that are like each other in some way. Work out which of the five figures on the right is most like the three figures on the left.

Example:

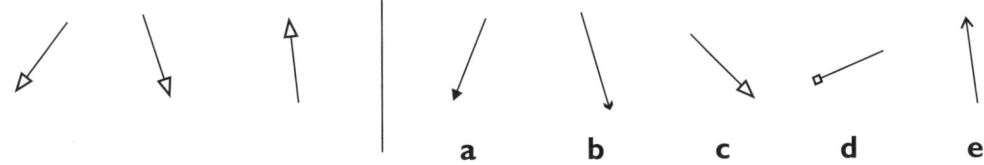

Answer: c

1

   |

a b c d e

2

 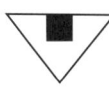  |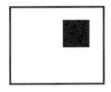

a b c d e

3

   |

a b c d e

4

   |

a b c d e

5

   |

a b c d e

/ 5   Total   / 28

End of Test

Assessment Test 2

Assessment Test 3

You can print **multiple-choice answer sheets** for these questions from our website — go to cgpbooks.co.uk/11plus/answer-sheets or scan the QR code on the right. If you'd prefer to answer them in standard write-in format, just circle the letter underneath your answer. The test should take around 15 minutes.

Section 1 — Find the Figure Like the First Two

In each question, there are two figures on the left that are like each other in some way. Work out which of the five figures on the right is most like the two figures on the left.

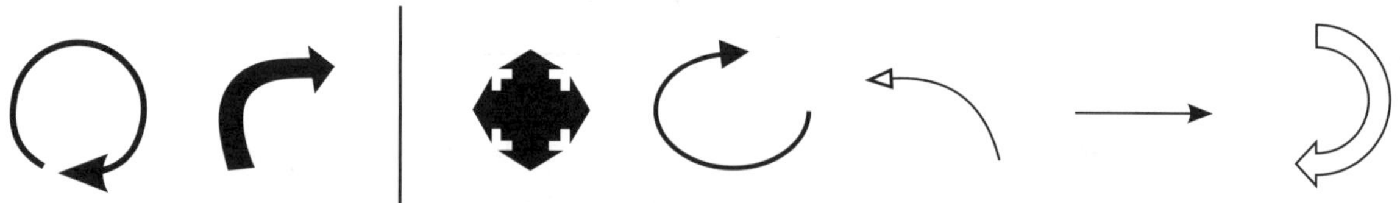

Example: *(shown with)* **Answer: c**

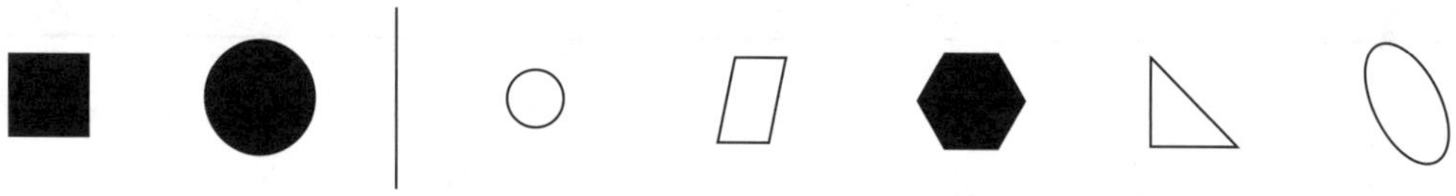

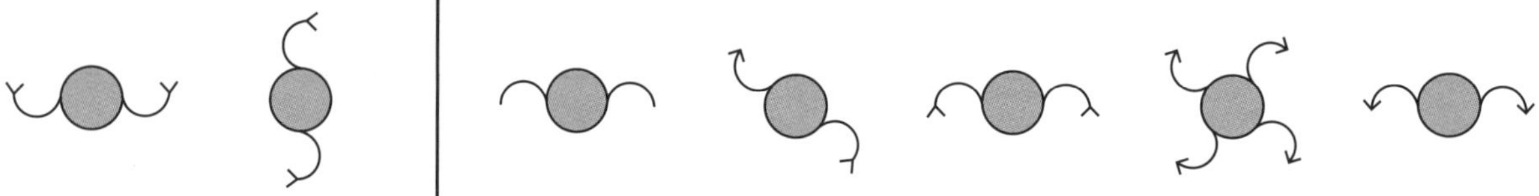

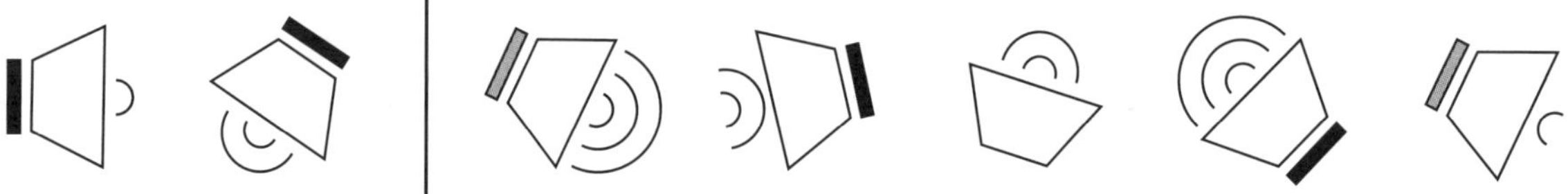

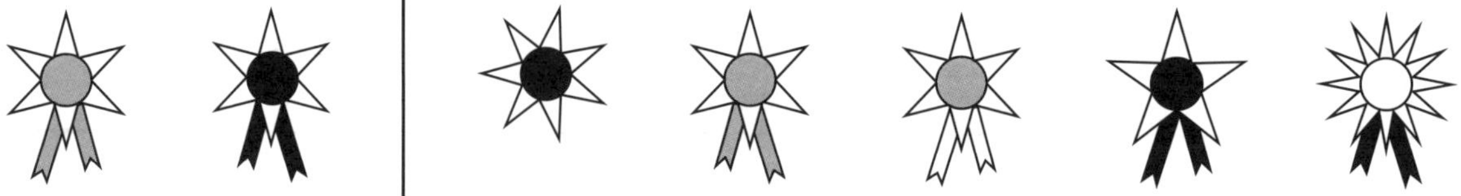

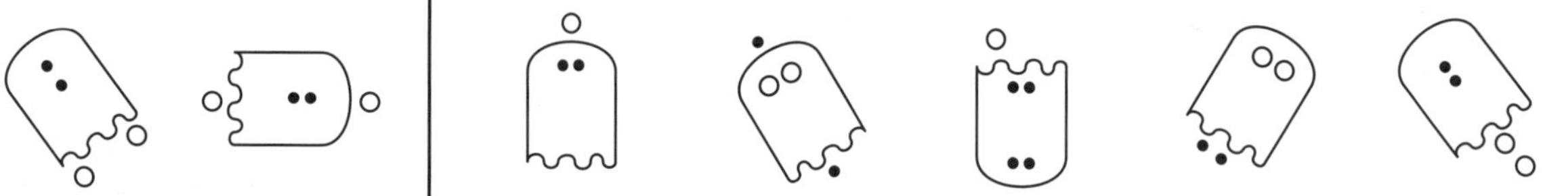

Section 2 — Vertical Code

Each question has three figures on the left with code letters that describe them. You need to work out what the code letters mean. The figure on the right is missing its code. Work out which of the five codes on the right describes this figure.

Example:  P

⇧ Q

⇦ R

⇨   P   Q   T   S   R
       a   b   c   d   e

Answer: a

The arrow pointing right has the code letter P. The arrow pointing up has the code letter Q. The arrow pointing left has the code letter R. The figure on the right is an arrow pointing right, so its code must be P and the answer is **a**.

1)  F

 H

 G

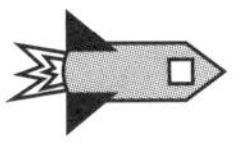

    K   H   F   G   J
             a   b   c   d   e

2)  HZ

 JY

 HY

    HY   JZ   HZ   JX   JY
            a   b   c   d   e

3) AV

 BW

 CV

    CW   AV   BV   CV   AW
            a   b   c   d   e

4)  CY

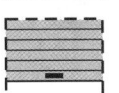 DX

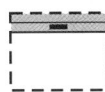 BX

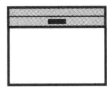   DY   BX   CX   BY   DX
            a   b   c   d   e

/ 4

Carry on to the next question → →

Assessment Test 3

Section 3 — Complete the Series

Each of these questions has five squares on the left that are arranged in order. One of the squares is empty. Work out which of the five squares on the right should replace the empty square.

Example: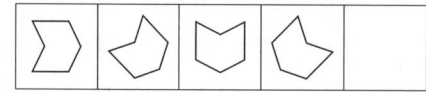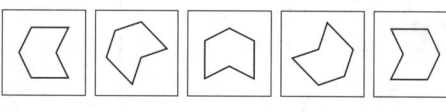

Answer: a

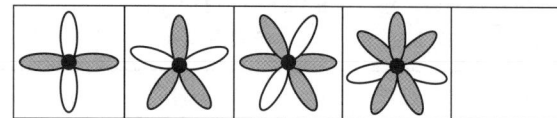 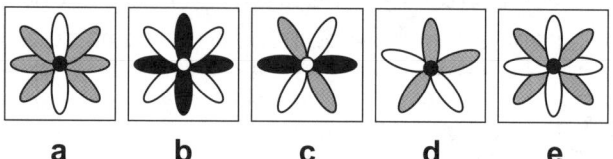

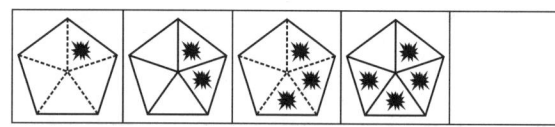 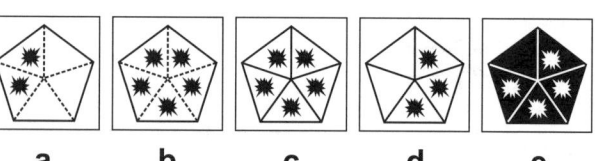

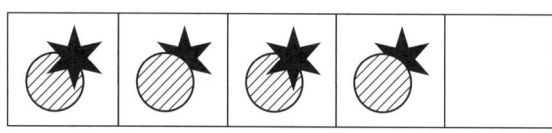 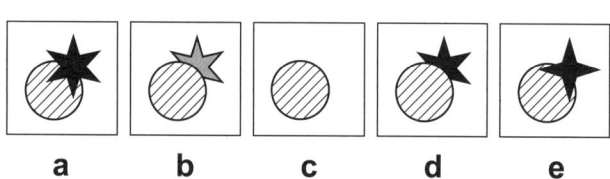

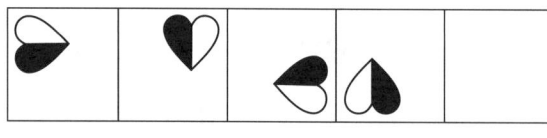 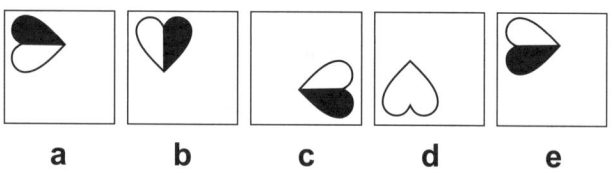

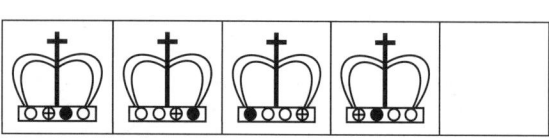 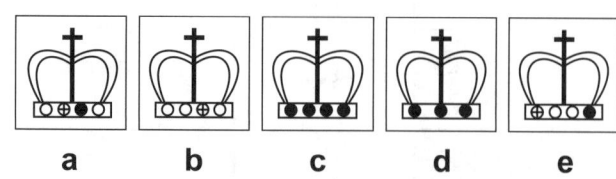

Assessment Test 3

Section 4 — Complete the Grid

On the left of each question below is a grid with one empty square.
Work out which of the five squares on the right should replace the empty square.

Example:

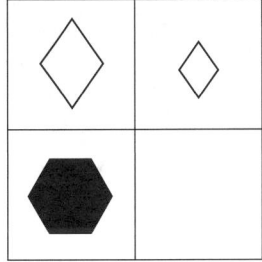 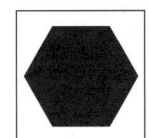   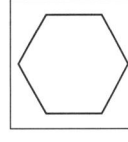 

a · b · c · d · e

Answer: c

1

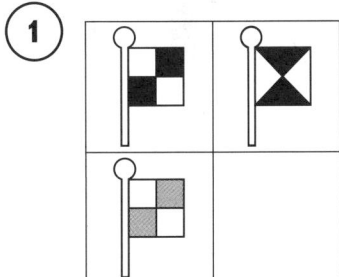 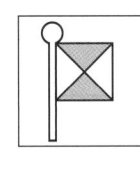 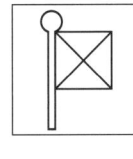 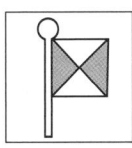  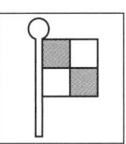

a · b · c · d · e

2

a · b · c · d · e

3

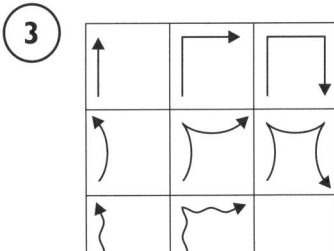 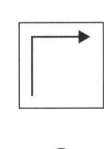 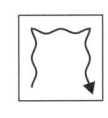 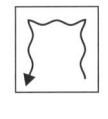 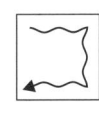 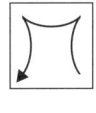

a · b · c · d · e

4

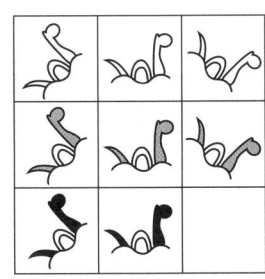     

a · b · c · d · e

Carry on to the next question → →

Assessment Test 3

Section 5 — Complete the Pair

The first figure in each question changes to become the second figure. Work out how the first figure has been changed. Then find the figure on the right that would match the third figure if it was changed in the same way.

Example:

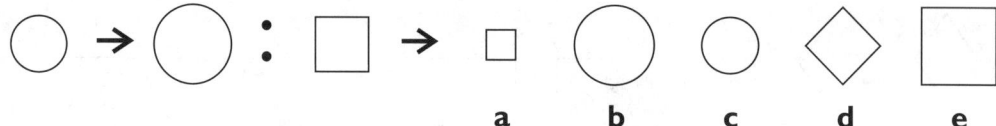

Answer: e

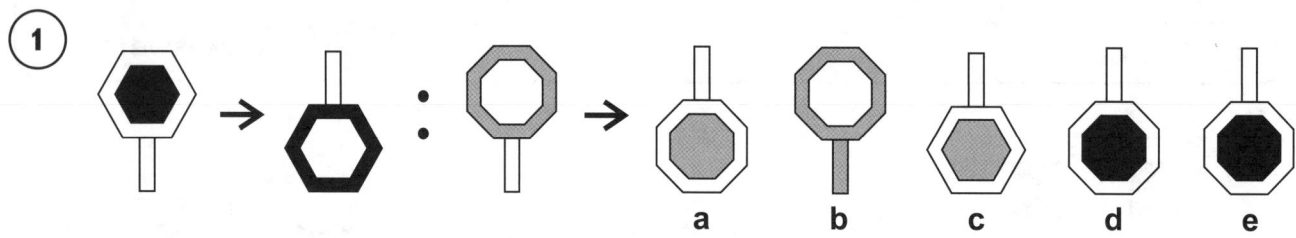

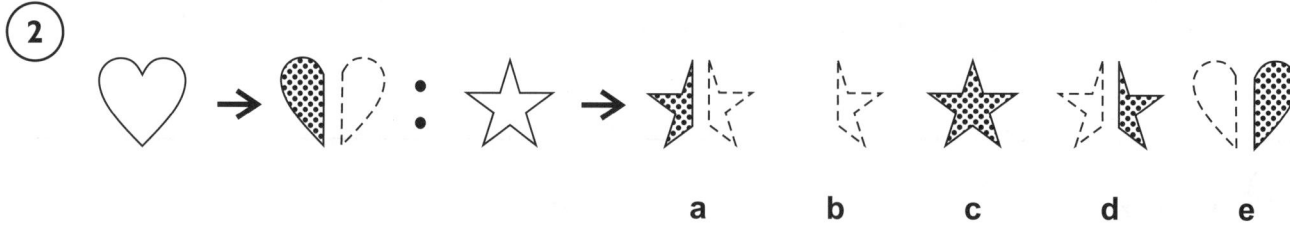

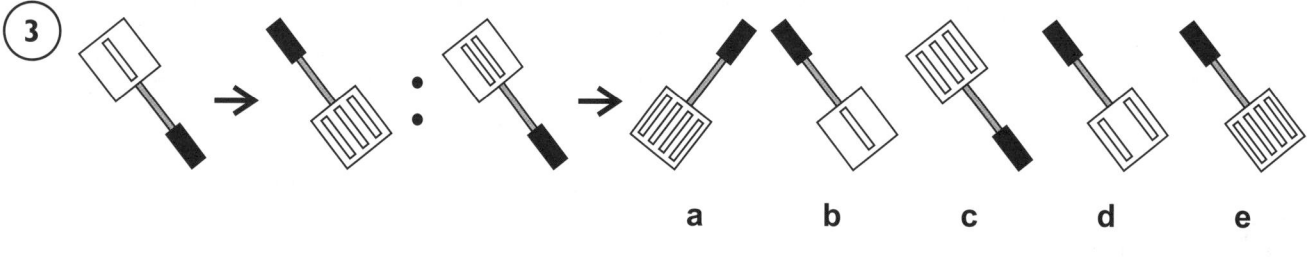

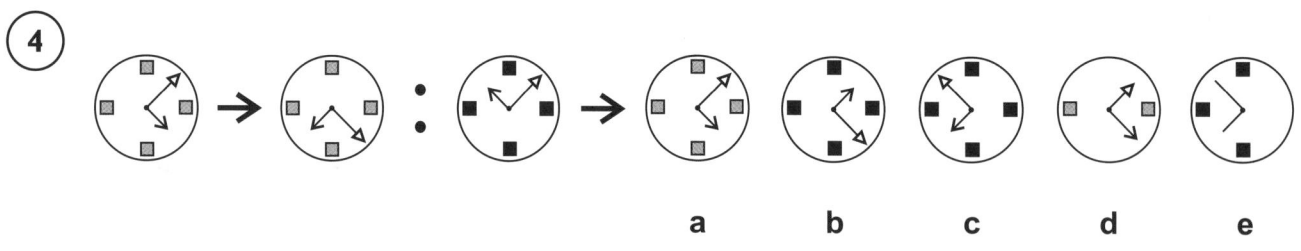

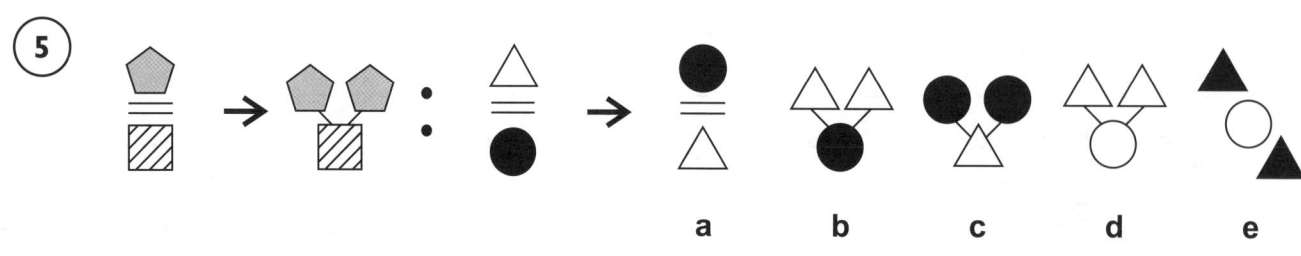

Section 6 — Odd One Out

Each of the questions below has five figures.
Find the figure in each row that is most unlike the others.

Example:

 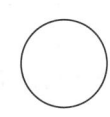   
a b c d e

Answer: b

a b c d e

a b c d e

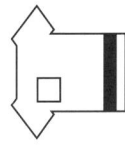 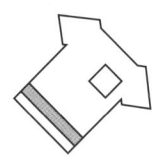  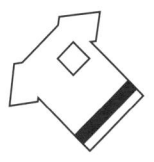 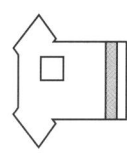
a b c d e

a b c d e

 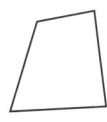 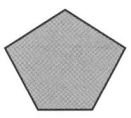  
a b c d e

/ 5   Total / 28

End of Test

Assessment Test 3

Assessment Test 4

You can print **multiple-choice answer sheets** for these questions from our website — go to cgpbooks.co.uk/11plus/answer-sheets or scan the QR code on the right. If you'd prefer to answer them in standard write-in format, just circle the letter underneath your answer. The test should take around 15 minutes.

Section 1 — Complete the Series

Each of these questions has five squares on the left that are arranged in order. One of the squares is empty. Work out which of the five squares on the right should replace the empty square.

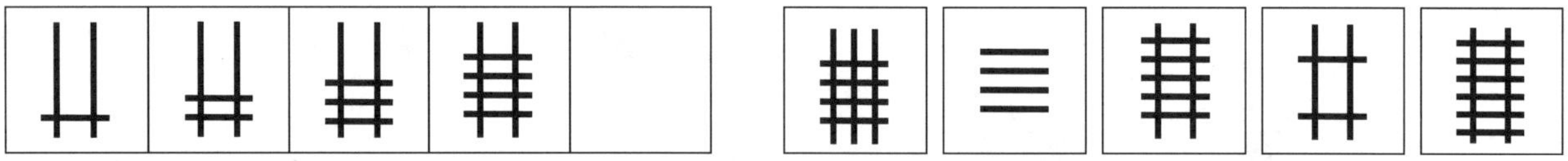

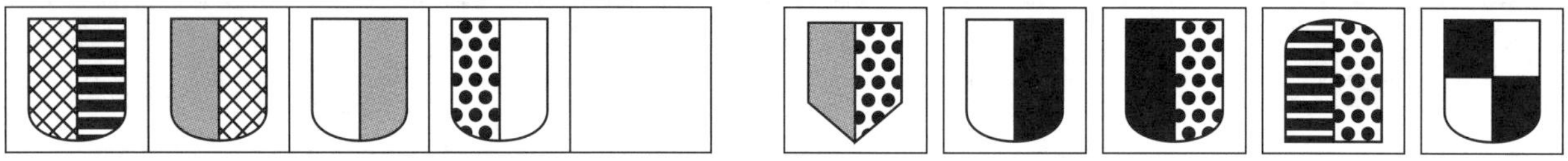

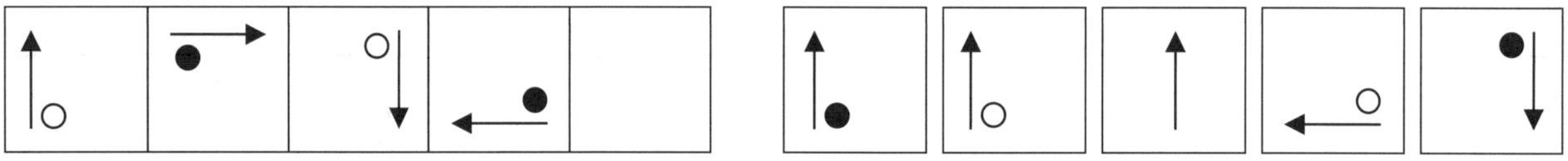

Example:

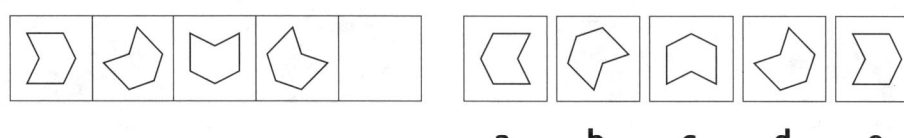

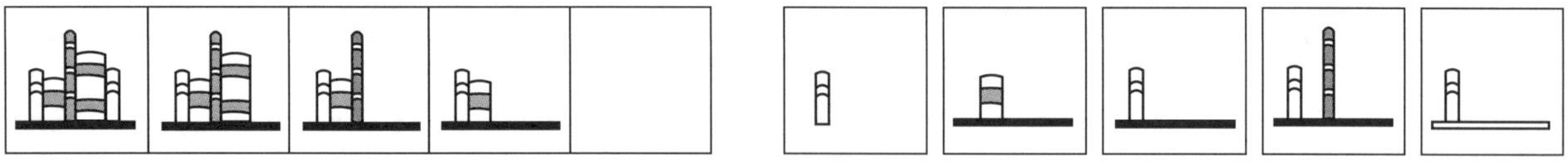

Answer: a

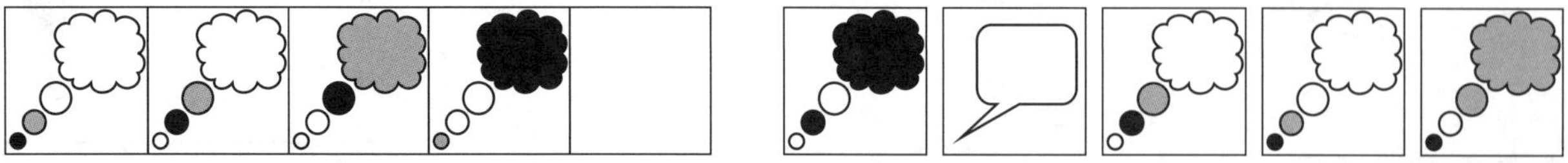

Section 2 — Complete the Grid

On the left of each question below is a grid with one empty square.
Work out which of the five squares on the right should replace the empty square.

Example:

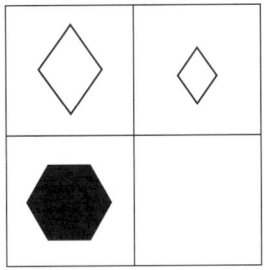    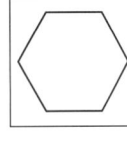 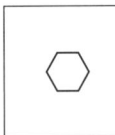

a　　b　　c　　d　　e

Answer: **c**

1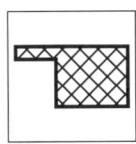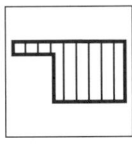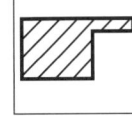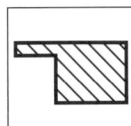

a　　b　　c　　d　　e

2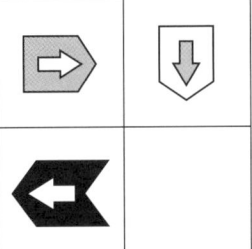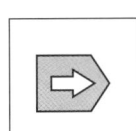

a　　b　　c　　d　　e

3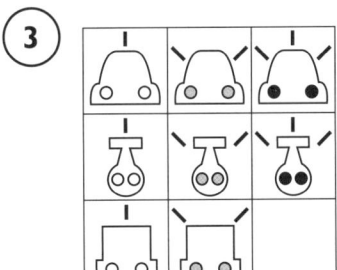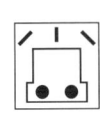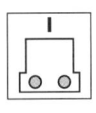

a　　b　　c　　d　　e

4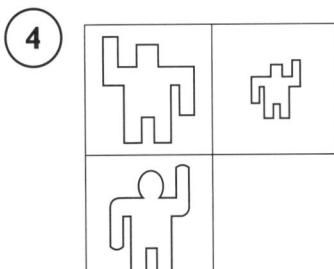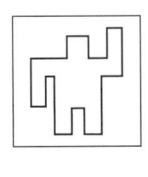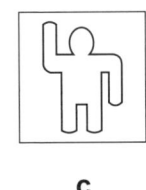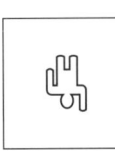

a　　b　　c　　d　　e

/ 4

Carry on to the next question →→

Assessment Test 4

Section 3 — Find the Figure Like the First Three

In each question, there are three figures on the left that are like each other in some way. Work out which of the five figures on the right is most like the three figures on the left.

Example:

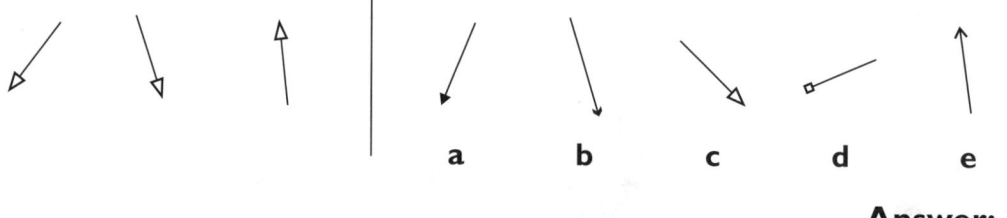

Answer: c

(1)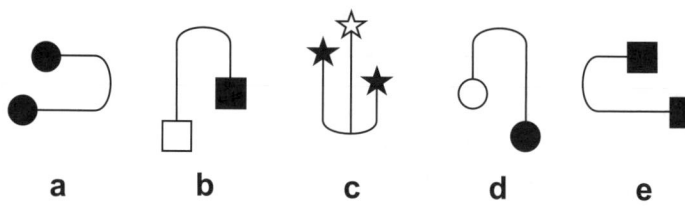

(2)
a b c d e

(3)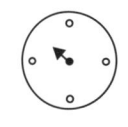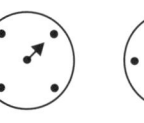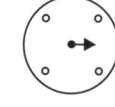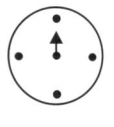
a b c d e

(4)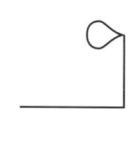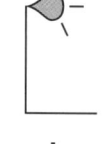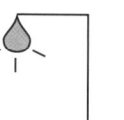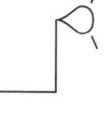
a b c d e

(5)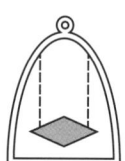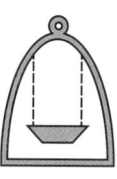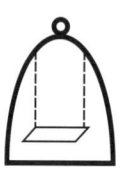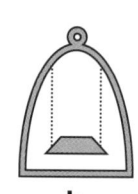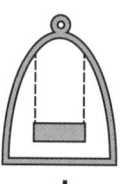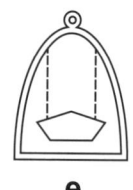
a b c d e

/ 5

Assessment Test 4

Section 4 — Odd One Out

Each of the questions below has five figures.
Find the figure in each row that is most unlike the others.

Example:

a   b   c   d   e

Answer: b

(1)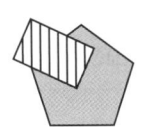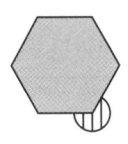

a   b   c   d   e

(2)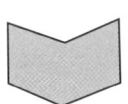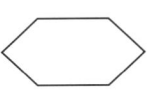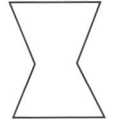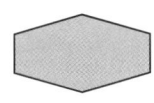

a   b   c   d   e

(3)

a   b   c   d   e

(4)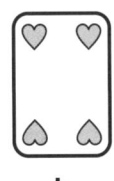

a   b   c   d   e

(5)

a   b   c   d   e

/ 5

Carry on to the next question → →

Assessment Test 4

Section 5 — Vertical Code

Each question has three figures on the left with code letters that describe them. You need to work out what the code letters mean. The figure on the right is missing its code. Work out which of the five codes on the right describes this figure.

Example:

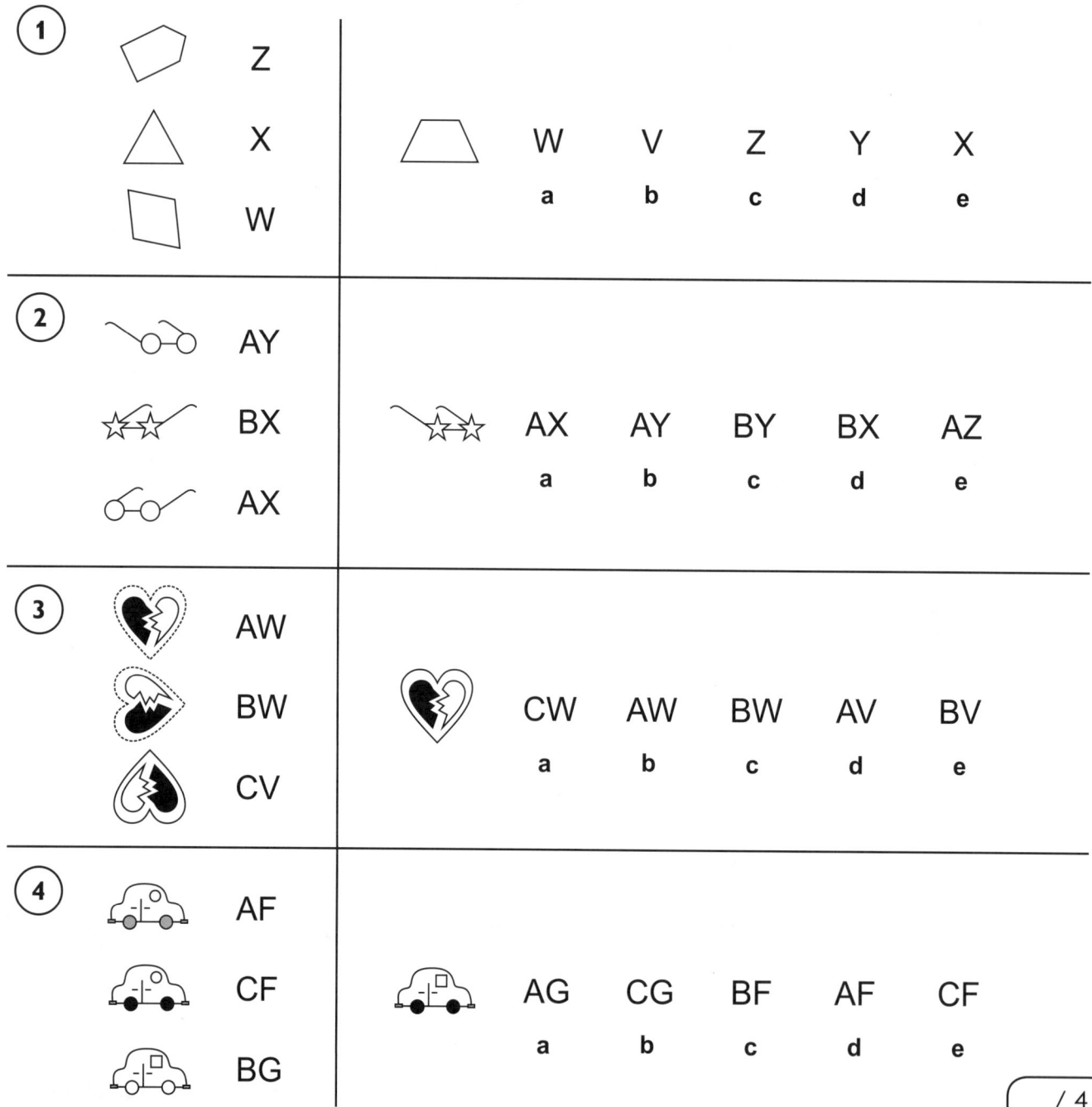

Answer: a

The arrow pointing right has the code letter P. The arrow pointing up has the code letter Q. The arrow pointing left has the code letter R. The figure on the right is an arrow pointing right, so its code must be P and the answer is **a**.

Assessment Test 4

Section 6 — Complete the Pair

The first figure in each question changes to become the second figure. Work out how the first figure has been changed. Then find the figure on the right that would match the third figure if it was changed in the same way.

Example:

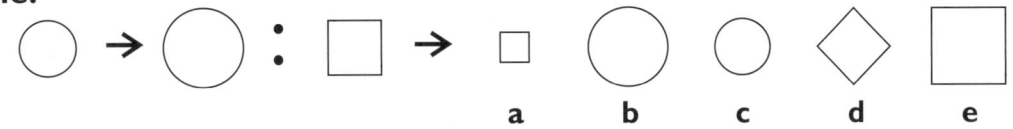

Answer: e

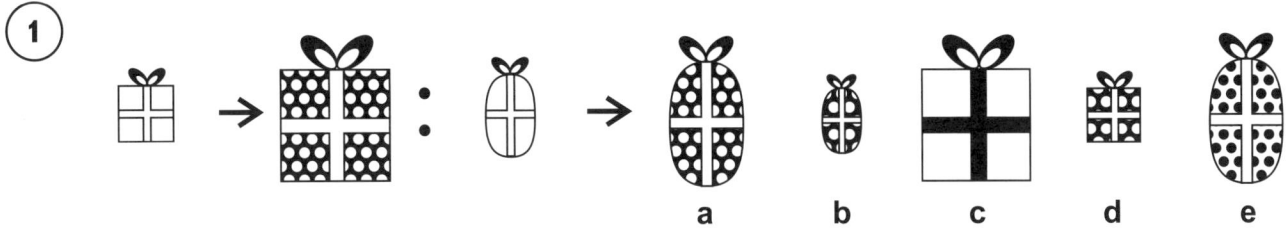

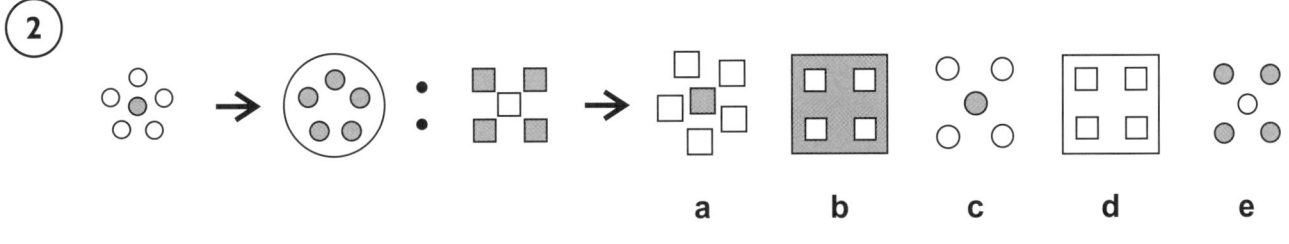

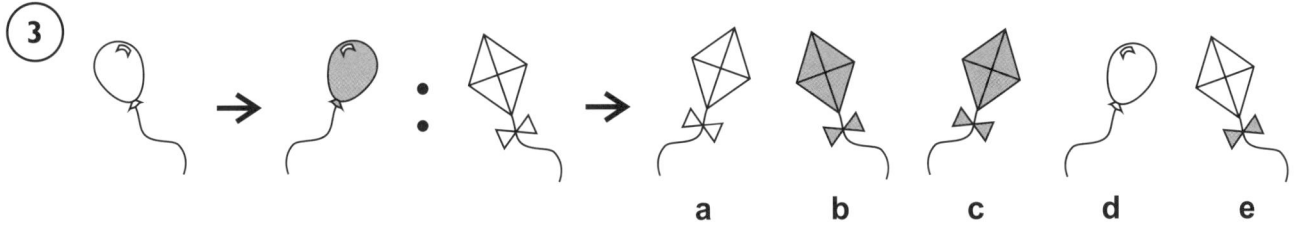

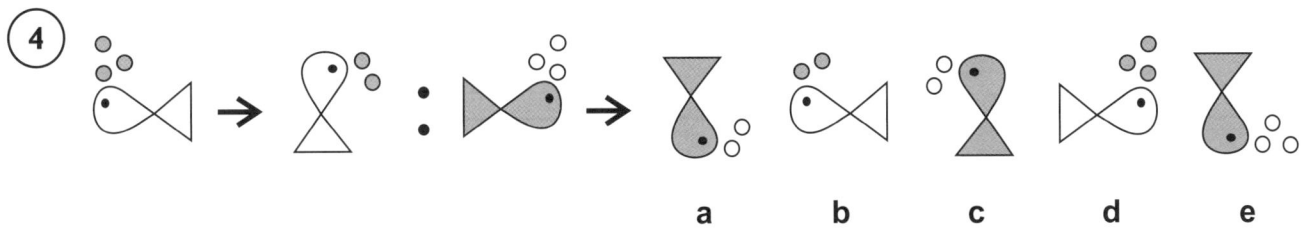

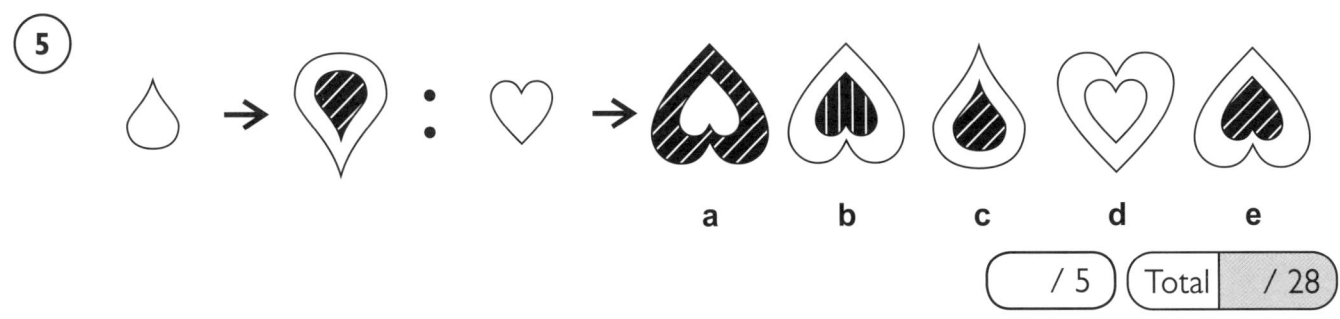

End of Test

Assessment Test 5

You can print **multiple-choice answer sheets** for these questions from our website — go to cgpbooks.co.uk/11plus/answer-sheets or scan the QR code on the right. If you'd prefer to answer them in standard write-in format, just circle the letter underneath your answer. The test should take around 15 minutes.

Section 1 — Complete the Pair

The first figure in each question changes to become the second figure. Work out how the first figure has been changed. Then find the figure on the right that would match the third figure if it was changed in the same way.

Example:

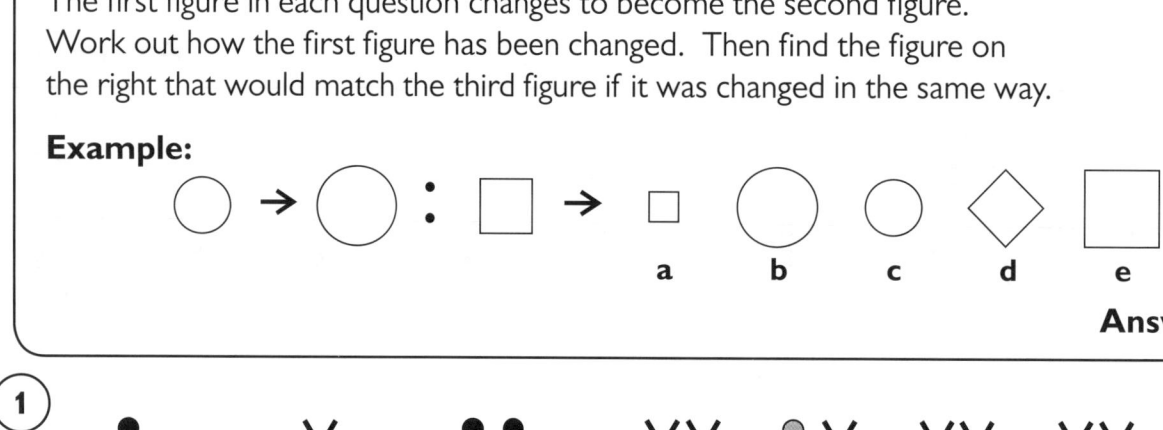

Answer: e

1.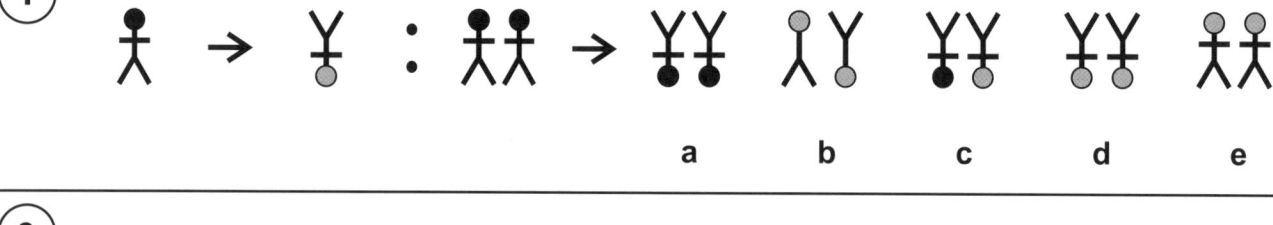

2.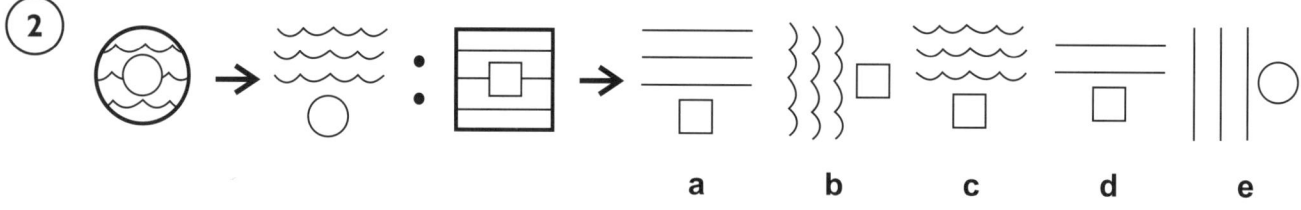

3.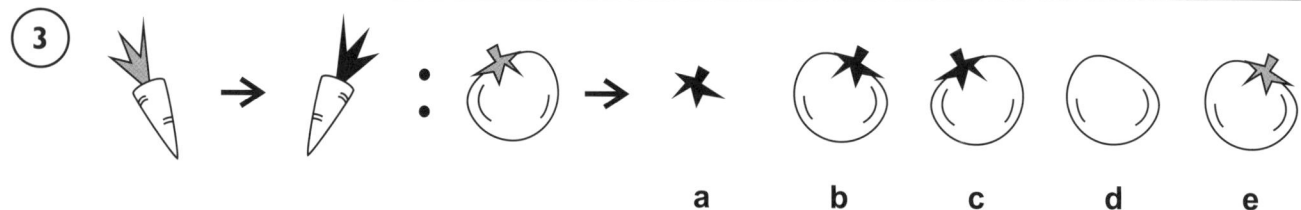

4.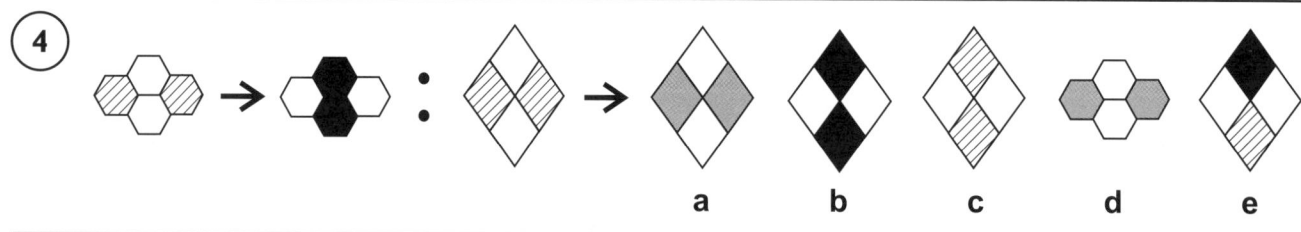

5.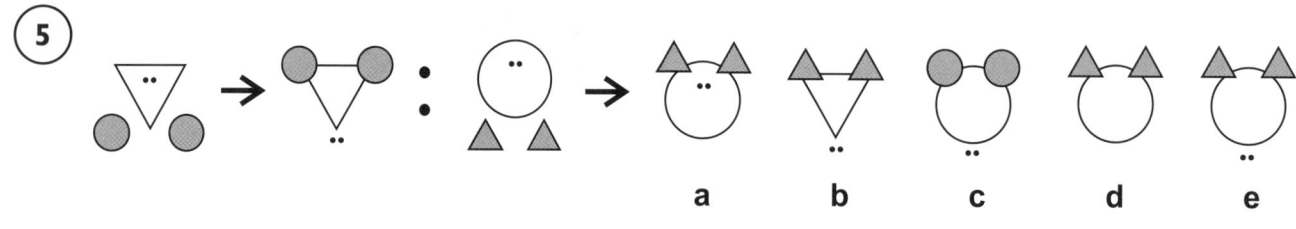

/ 5

Section 2 — Odd One Out

Each of the questions below has five figures.
Find the figure in each row that is most unlike the others.

Example:

 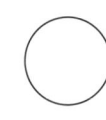   
a b c d e

Answer: b

1
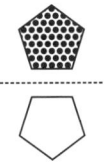 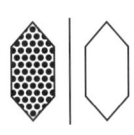 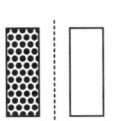  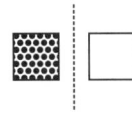
a b c d e

2
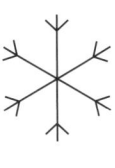 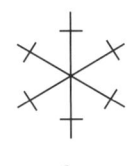 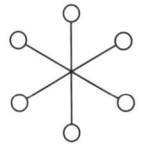 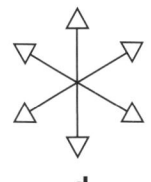 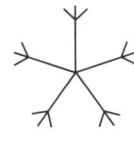
a b c d e

3

a b c d e

4
 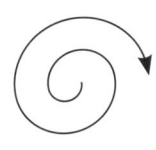 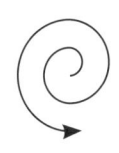  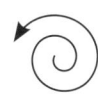
a b c d e

5

a b c d e

/ 5

Carry on to the next question →→

Assessment Test 5

Section 3 — Vertical Code

Each question has three figures on the left with code letters that describe them. You need to work out what the code letters mean. The figure on the right is missing its code. Work out which of the five codes on the right describes this figure.

Example:

⇨	P
⇧	Q
⇦	R

⇨	P	Q	T	S	R
	a	b	c	d	e

Answer: a

The arrow pointing right has the code letter P. The arrow pointing up has the code letter Q. The arrow pointing left has the code letter R. The figure on the right is an arrow pointing right, so its code must be P and the answer is **a**.

1.

(two tall black posts)	AX
(two short posts with caps)	BY
(one tall one short)	AY

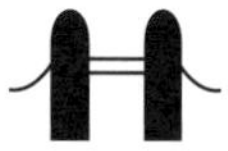	AX	AY	BX	BY	BZ
	a	b	c	d	e

2.

(right arrow, one barb)	GK
(left arrow, double barb)	HL
(left arrow, single barb)	HK

	HL	GK	HM	GH	GL
	a	b	c	d	e

3.

(spiral with dot top)	EN
(spiral with dot left)	DN
(spiral with dot bottom)	CM

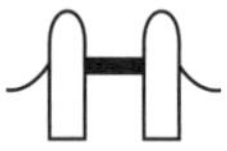

	EN	EM	DM	CN	CM
	a	b	c	d	e

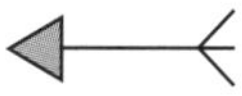

4.

(moon with 2 stars)	XC
(moon with 1 star)	WC
(moon with 3 stars)	YD

	XD	YC	WC	XC	YD
	a	b	c	d	e

/ 4

Assessment Test 5

Section 4 — Complete the Grid

On the left of each question below is a grid with one empty square.
Work out which of the five squares on the right should replace the empty square.

Example:

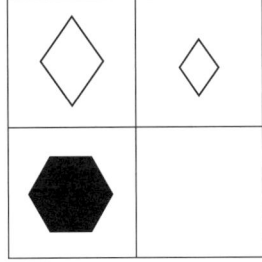 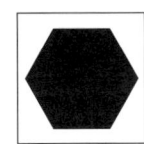 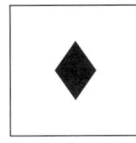 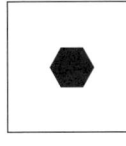 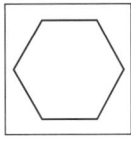 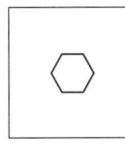

a　　　b　　　c　　　d　　　e

Answer: c

(1)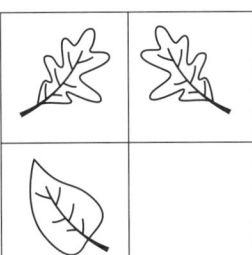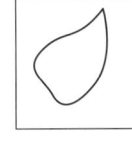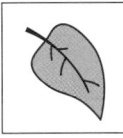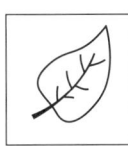

a　　　b　　　c　　　d　　　e

(2)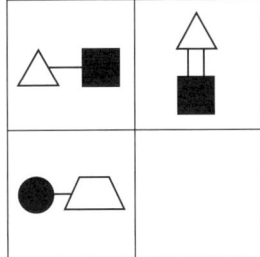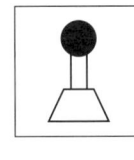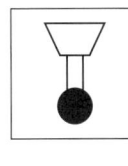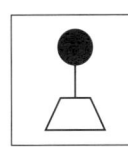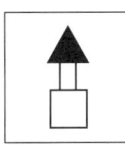

a　　　b　　　c　　　d　　　e

(3)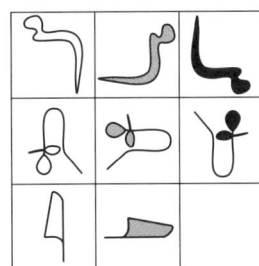

a　　　b　　　c　　　d　　　e

(4)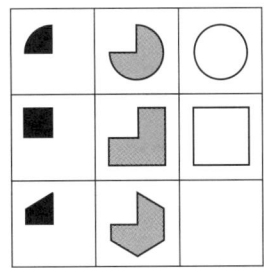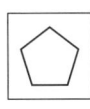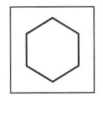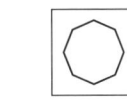

a　　　b　　　c　　　d　　　e

Carry on to the next question → →

Assessment Test 5

Section 5 — Find the Figure Like the First Two

In each question, there are two figures on the left that are like each other in some way. Work out which of the five figures on the right is most like the two figures on the left.

Example:

  |

                                      a   b   c   d   e

Answer: c

1   |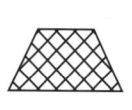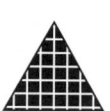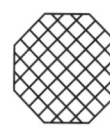

                                      a   b   c   d   e

2 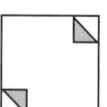 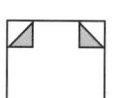 |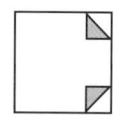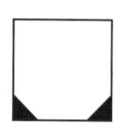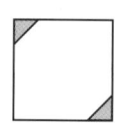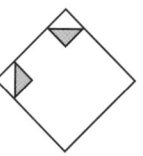

                                      a   b   c   d   e

3  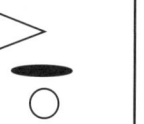 |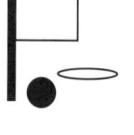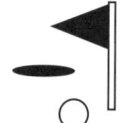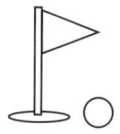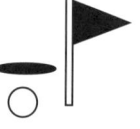

                                      a   b   c   d   e

4 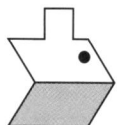  |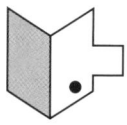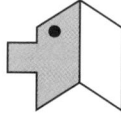

                                      a   b   c   d   e

5   |

                                      a   b   c   d   e

/ 5

Assessment Test 5

Section 6 — Complete the Series

Each of these questions has five squares on the left that are arranged in order. One of the squares is empty. Work out which of the five squares on the right should replace the empty square.

Example: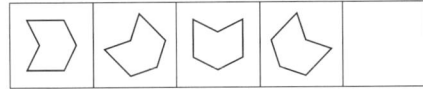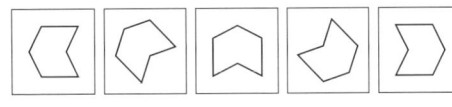

Answer: a

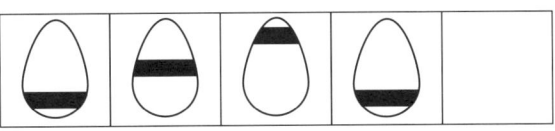 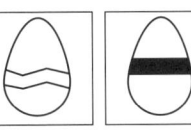   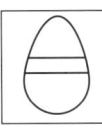

  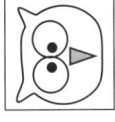  

3
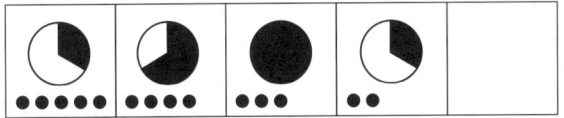   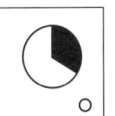 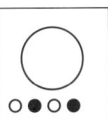 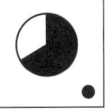

4
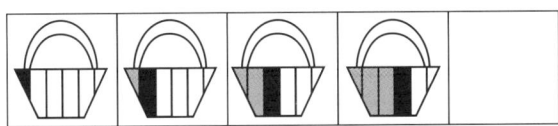     

5
 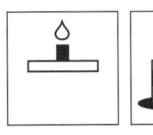   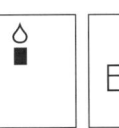 

/ 5 Total / 28

End of Test

Assessment Test 5

Assessment Test 6

You can print **multiple-choice answer sheets** for these questions from our website — go to cgpbooks.co.uk/11plus/answer-sheets or scan the QR code on the right. If you'd prefer to answer them in standard write-in format, just circle the letter underneath your answer. The test should take around 15 minutes.

Section 1 — Find the Figure Like the First Three

In each question, there are three figures on the left that are like each other in some way. Work out which of the five figures on the right is most like the three figures on the left.

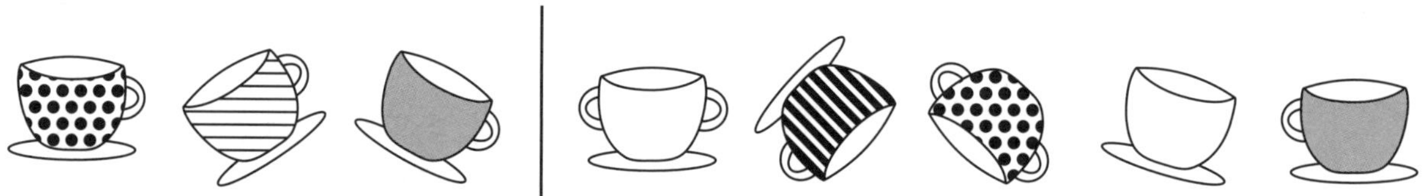

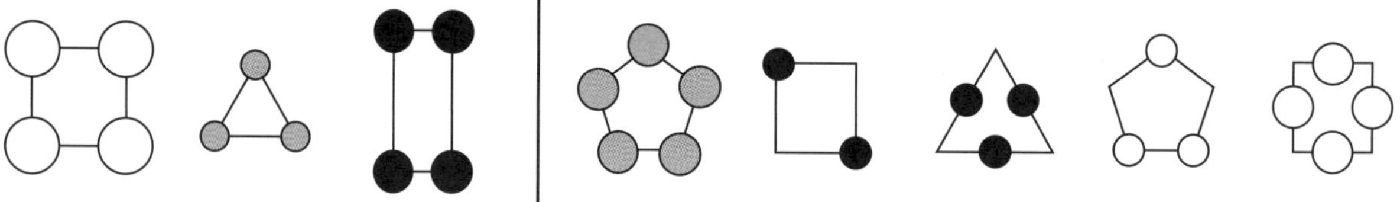

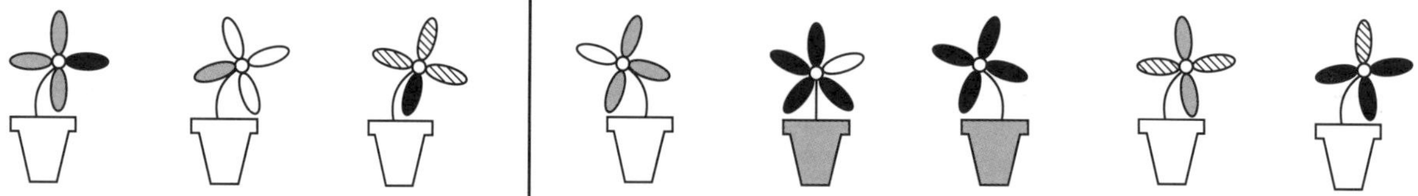

Example:

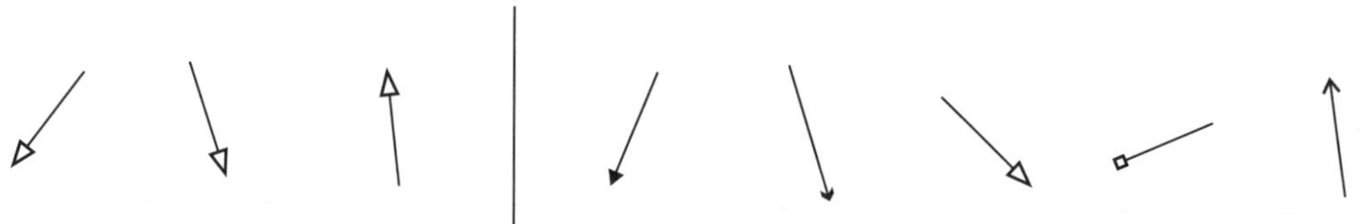

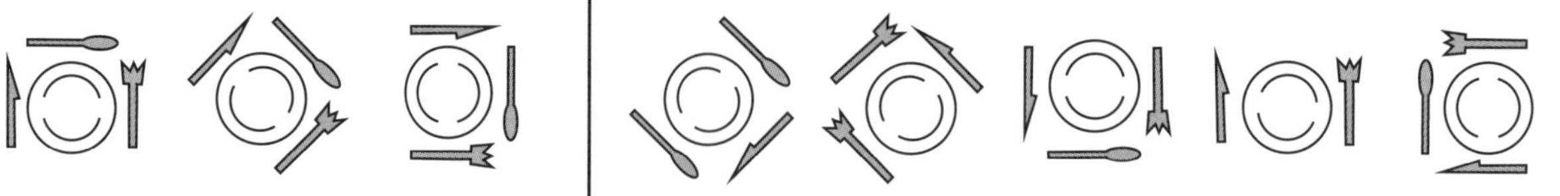

Answer: c

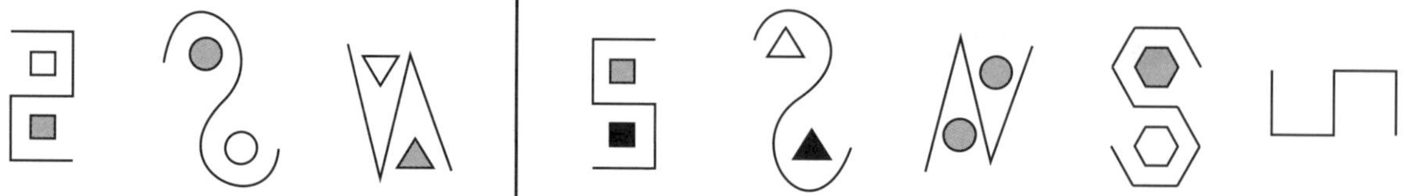

Section 2 — Complete the Series

Each of these questions has five squares on the left that are arranged in order. One of the squares is empty. Work out which of the five squares on the right should replace the empty square.

Example: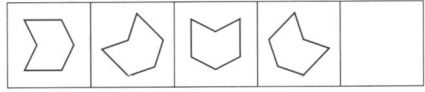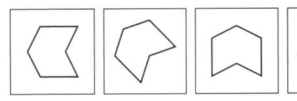

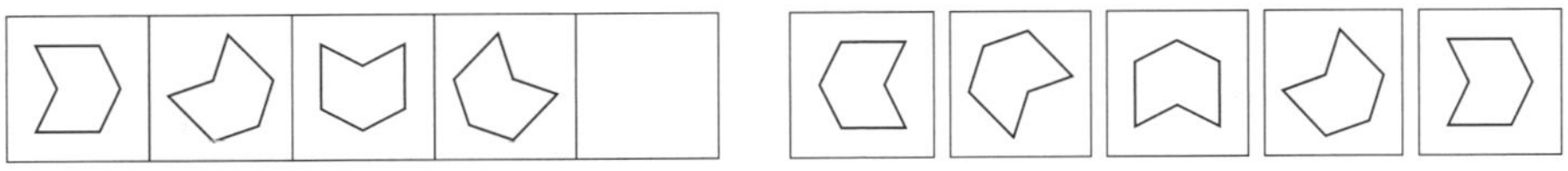

a b c d e

Answer: a

1)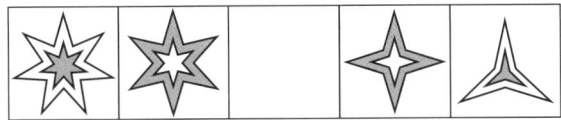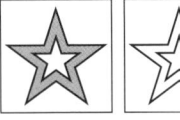

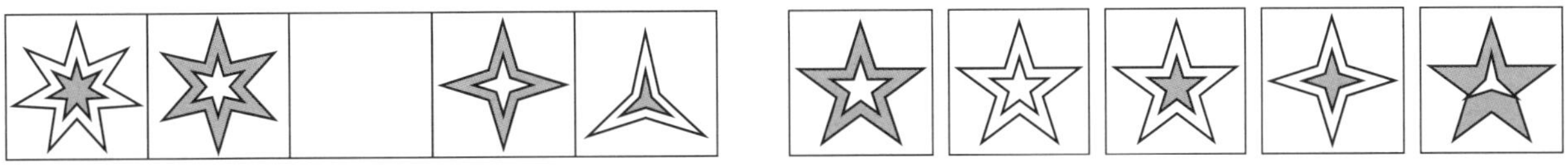

a b c d e

2)

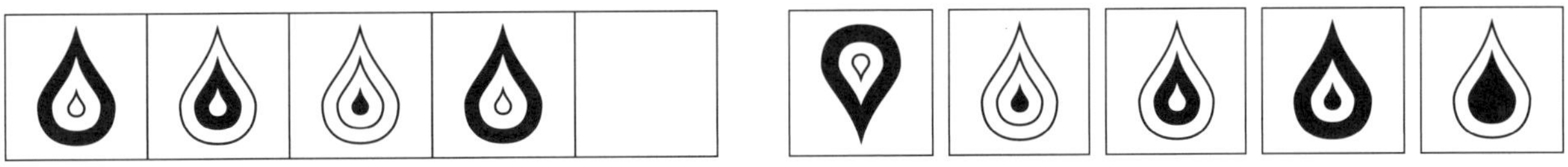

a b c d e

3)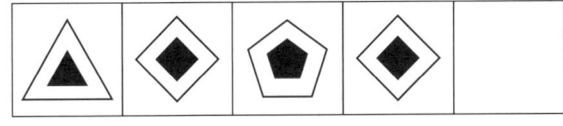

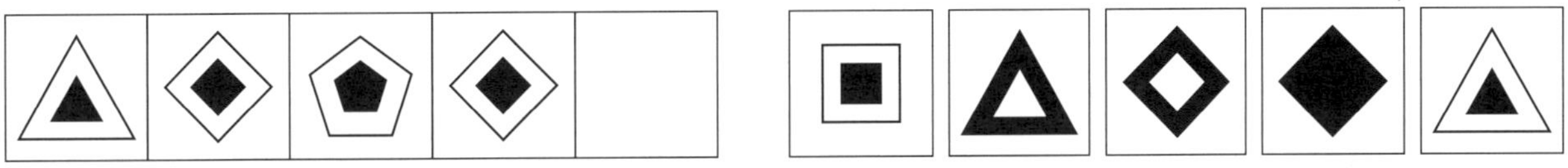

a b c d e

4)

a b c d e

5)

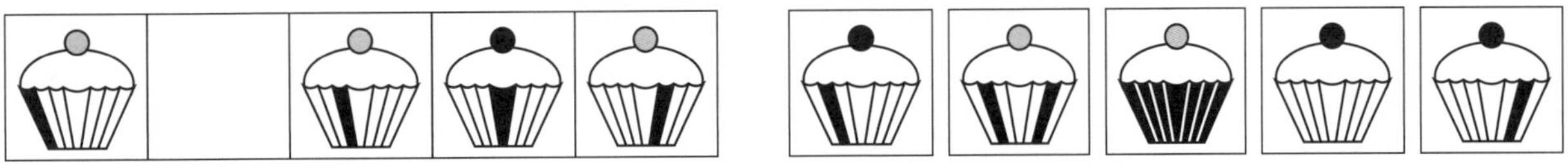

a b c d e

/ 5

Carry on to the next question → →

Assessment Test 6

Section 3 — Odd One Out

Each of the questions below has five figures.
Find the figure in each row that is most unlike the others.

Example:

a   b   c   d   e

Answer: b

1

a   b   c   d   e

2

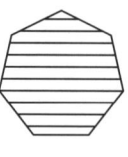         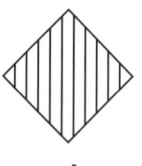   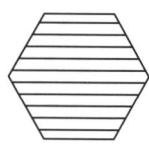

a   b   c   d   e

3

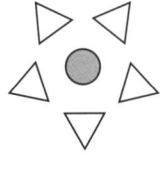      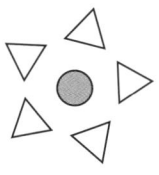   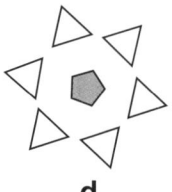   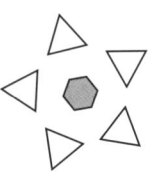

a   b   c   d   e

4

      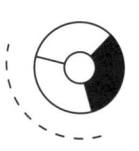   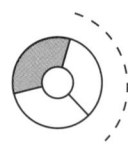   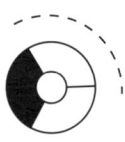

a   b   c   d   e

5

a   b   c   d   e

/ 5

Assessment Test 6

Section 4 — Complete the Pair

The first figure in each question changes to become the second figure. Work out how the first figure has been changed. Then find the figure on the right that would match the third figure if it was changed in the same way.

Example:

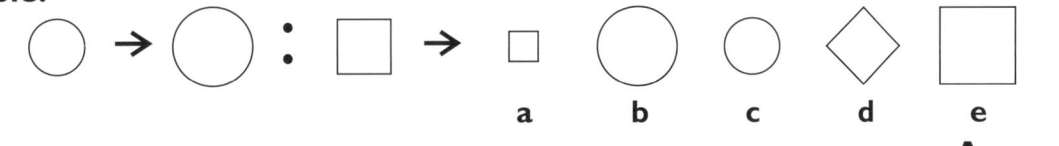

Answer: e

(1)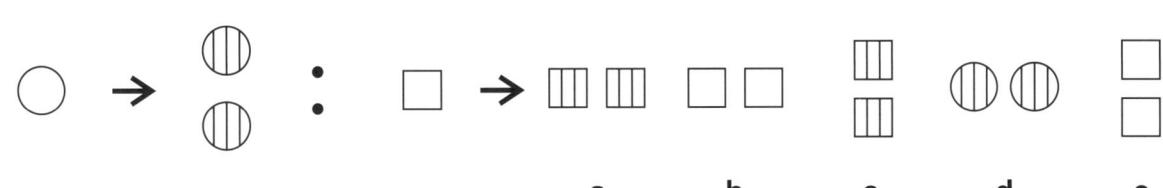

(2)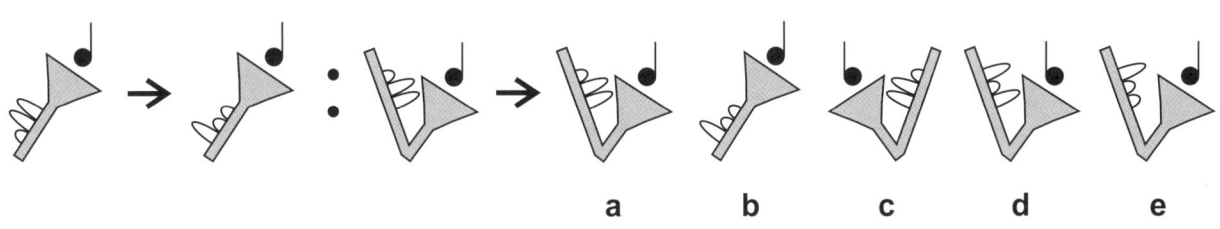

(3)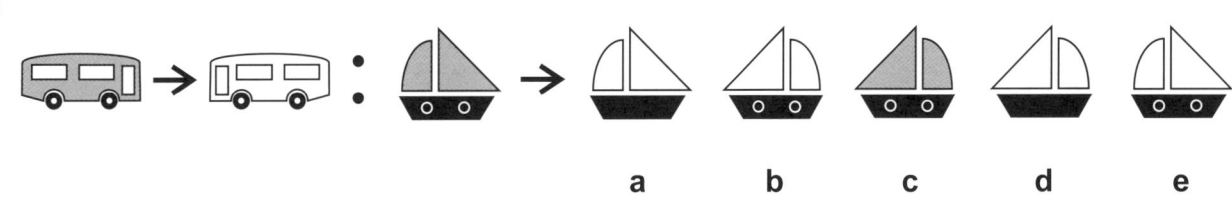

(4)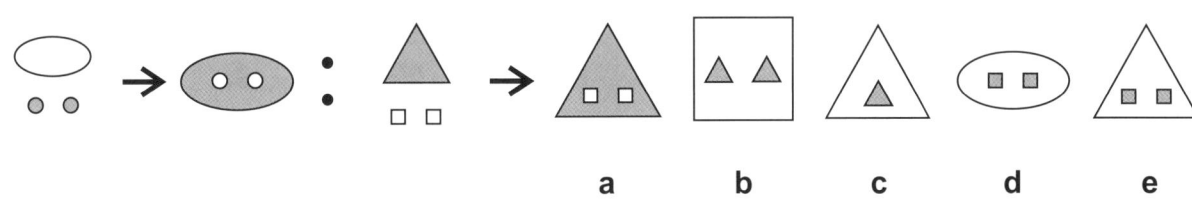

(5)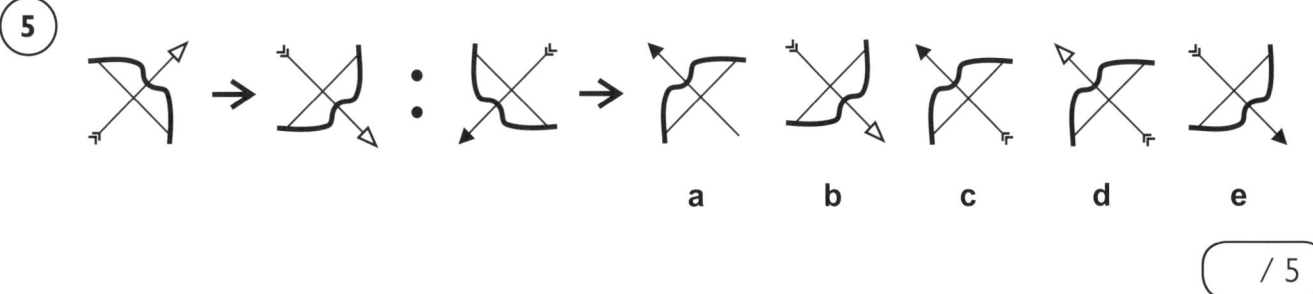

/ 5

Carry on to the next question → →

Assessment Test 6

Section 5 — Complete the Grid

On the left of each question below is a grid with one empty square.
Work out which of the five squares on the right should replace the empty square.

Example:

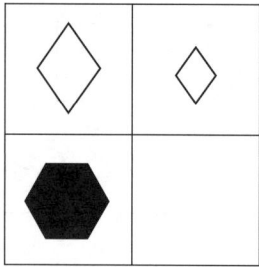    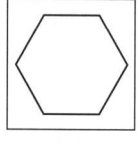 

a   b   c   d   e

Answer: c

①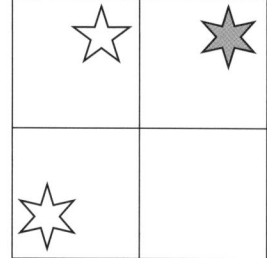

a   b   c   d   e

②

a   b   c   d   e

③

a   b   c   d   e

④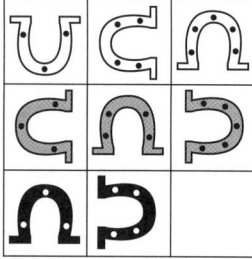

a   b   c   d   e

/ 4

Assessment Test 6

Section 6 — Vertical Code

Each question has three figures on the left with code letters that describe them. You need to work out what the code letters mean. The figure on the right is missing its code. Work out which of the five codes on the right describes this figure.

Example:

→ P		→	P	Q	T	S	R
↑ Q			a	b	c	d	e
← R						

Answer: a

The arrow pointing right has the code letter P. The arrow pointing up has the code letter Q. The arrow pointing left has the code letter R. The figure on the right is an arrow pointing right, so its code must be P and the answer is **a**.

1)
- ● CM 
- ○ DM 
- ■ DN

■ (outlined square) — CN(a) DM(b) CM(c) DP(d) DN(e)

2)
- party hat — RA
- party hat — SB
- party hat — RB

party hat — SB(a) RB(b) SA(c) RA(d) RC(e)

3)
- LP
- NQ
- MQ

— NP(a) MP(b) LQ(c) LP(d) MQ(e)

4)
- wheel — XF
- wheel — YG
- wheel — XE

wheel — XF(a) YE(b) XG(c) YG(d) YF(e)

/ 4   Total   / 28

End of Test

Assessment Test 6

Assessment Test 7

You can print **multiple-choice answer sheets** for these questions from our website — go to cgpbooks.co.uk/11plus/answer-sheets or scan the QR code on the right. If you'd prefer to answer them in standard write-in format, just circle the letter underneath your answer. The test should take around 15 minutes.

Section 1 — Odd One Out

Each of the questions below has five figures.
Find the figure in each row that is most unlike the others.

Example:

 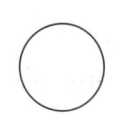   

a   b   c   d   e

Answer: b

(1)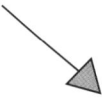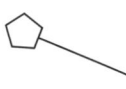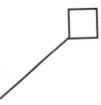

a   b   c   d   e

(2)

a   b   c   d   e

(3)

a   b   c   d   e

(4)

a   b   c   d   e

(5)   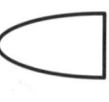

a   b   c   d   e

/ 5

Section 2 — Complete the Grid

On the left of each question below is a grid with one empty square.
Work out which of the five squares on the right should replace the empty square.

Example:

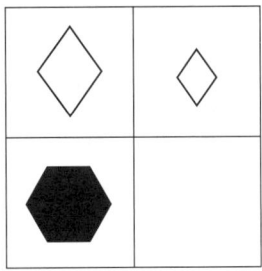    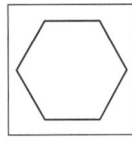 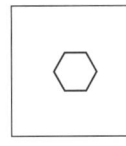

  a   b   c   d   e

Answer: c

1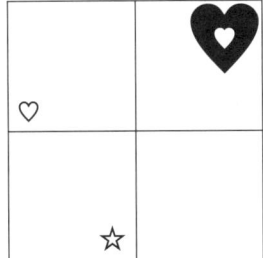

  a   b   c   d   e

2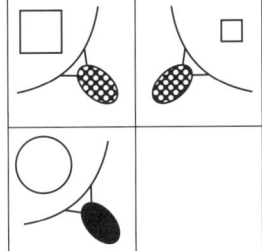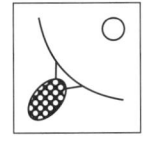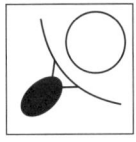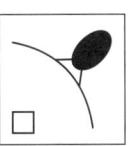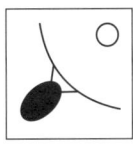

  a   b   c   d   e

3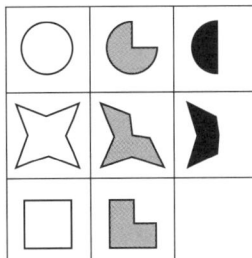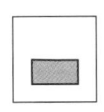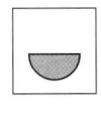

  a   b   c   d   e

4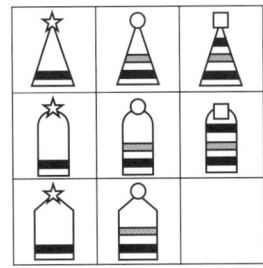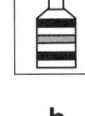

  a   b   c   d   e

/ 4

Carry on to the next question → →

Assessment Test 7

Section 3 — Complete the Pair

The first figure in each question changes to become the second figure. Work out how the first figure has been changed. Then find the figure on the right that would match the third figure if it was changed in the same way.

Example:

Answer: e

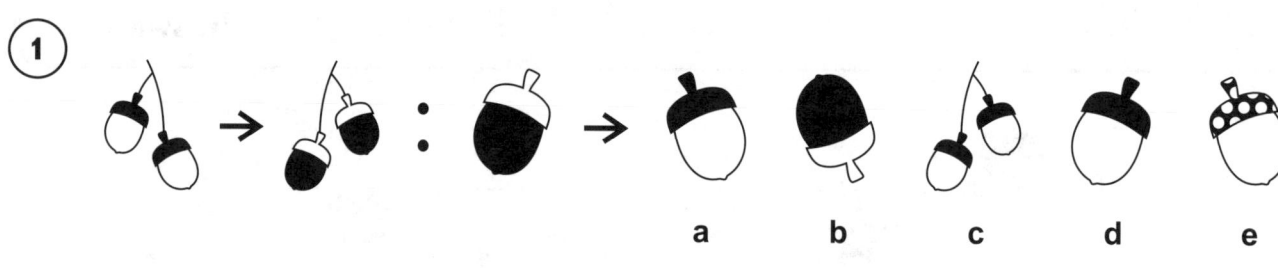

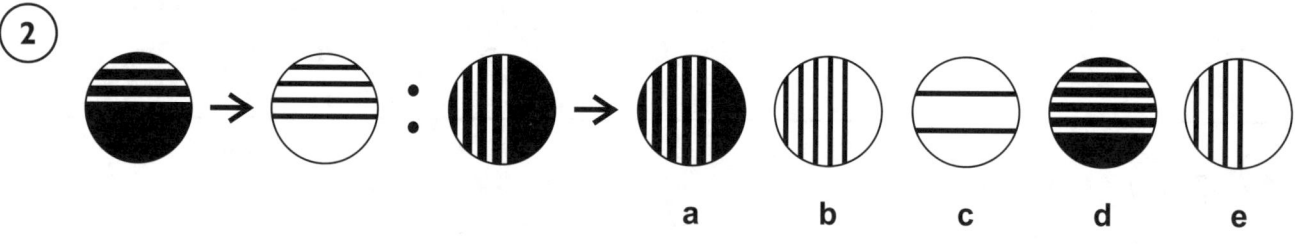

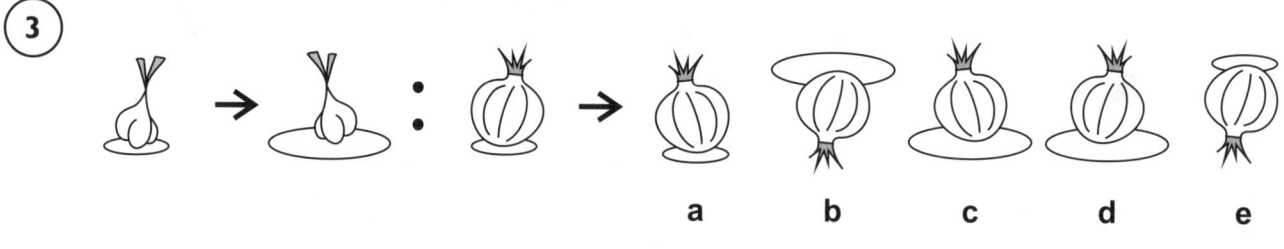

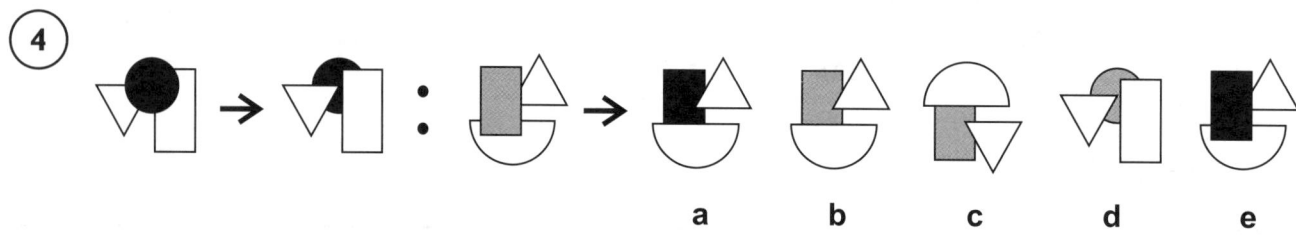

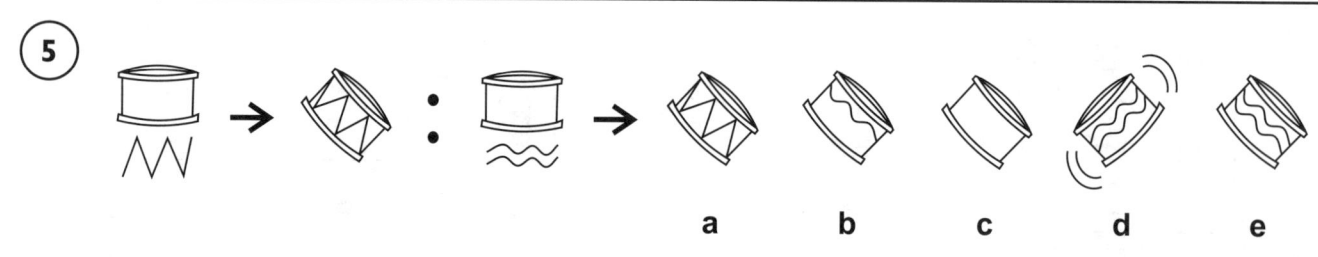

Assessment Test 7

Section 4 — Vertical Code

Each question has three figures on the left with code letters that describe them. You need to work out what the code letters mean. The figure on the right is missing its code. Work out which of the five codes on the right describes this figure.

Example:

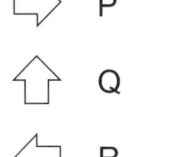

	P	Q	T	S	R
	a	b	c	d	e

Answer: a

The arrow pointing right has the code letter P. The arrow pointing up has the code letter Q. The arrow pointing left has the code letter R. The figure on the right is an arrow pointing right, so its code must be P and the answer is **a**.

---

1)

 AX

 BY

 BX

AX	BZ	AY	BX	BY
a	b	c	d	e

---

2)

 FP

 GP

 GQ

GQ	FQ	GP	FP	GR
a	b	c	d	e

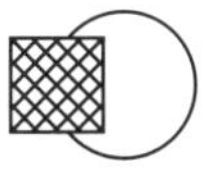

---

3)

 ZS

 XS

 YT

XS	ZS	YS	XT	ZT
a	b	c	d	e

---

4)

 VE

 VD

 WC

VC	WE	VD	WD	WC
a	b	c	d	e

/ 4

Carry on to the next question → →

Assessment Test 7

Section 5 — Complete the Series

Each of these questions has five squares on the left that are arranged in order. One of the squares is empty. Work out which of the five squares on the right should replace the empty square.

Example: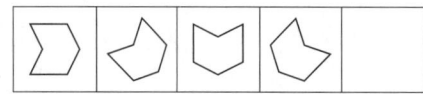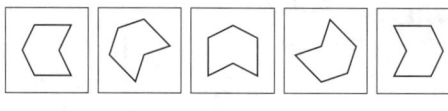

Answer: a

1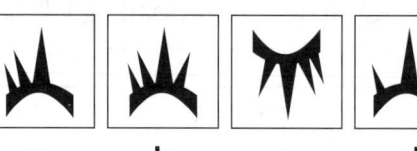

2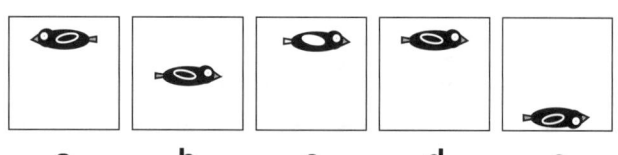

3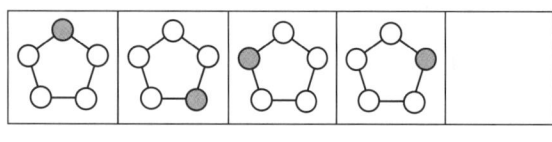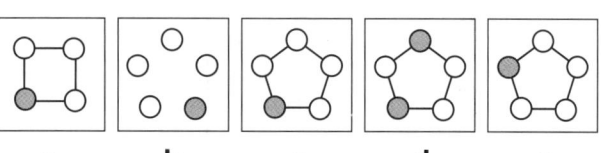

4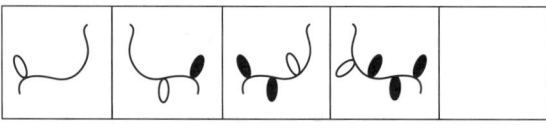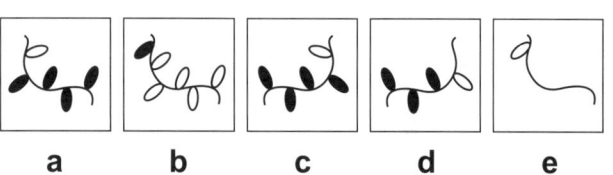

5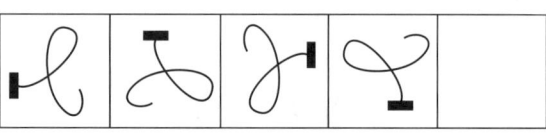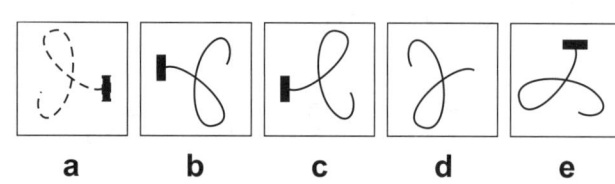

/ 5

Assessment Test 7

Section 6 — Find the Figure Like the First Two

In each question, there are two figures on the left that are like each other in some way. Work out which of the five figures on the right is most like the two figures on the left.

Example:

  |

                                            a   b   c   d   e

Answer: c

1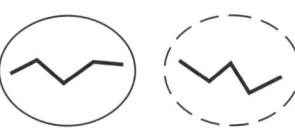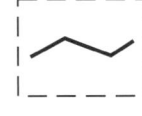

                                            a   b   c   d   e

2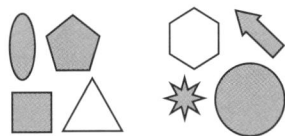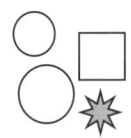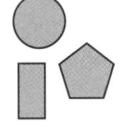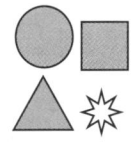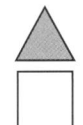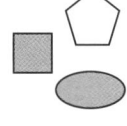

                                            a   b   c   d   e

3

                                            a   b   c   d   e

4

                                            a   b   c   d   e

5

                                            a   b   c   d   e

/ 5   Total   / 28

End of Test

Assessment Test 7

Assessment Test 8

You can print **multiple-choice answer sheets** for these questions from our website — go to cgpbooks.co.uk/11plus/answer-sheets or scan the QR code on the right. If you'd prefer to answer them in standard write-in format, just circle the letter underneath your answer. The test should take around 15 minutes.

Section 1 — Complete the Pair

The first figure in each question changes to become the second figure. Work out how the first figure has been changed. Then find the figure on the right that would match the third figure if it was changed in the same way.

Example:

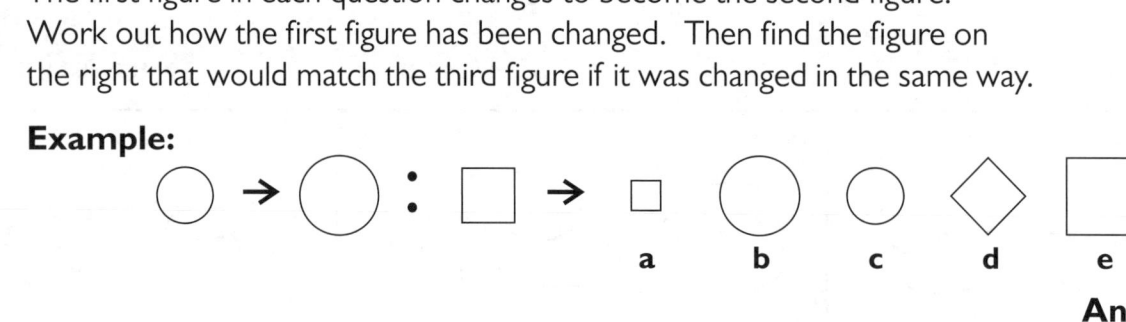

Answer: e

1.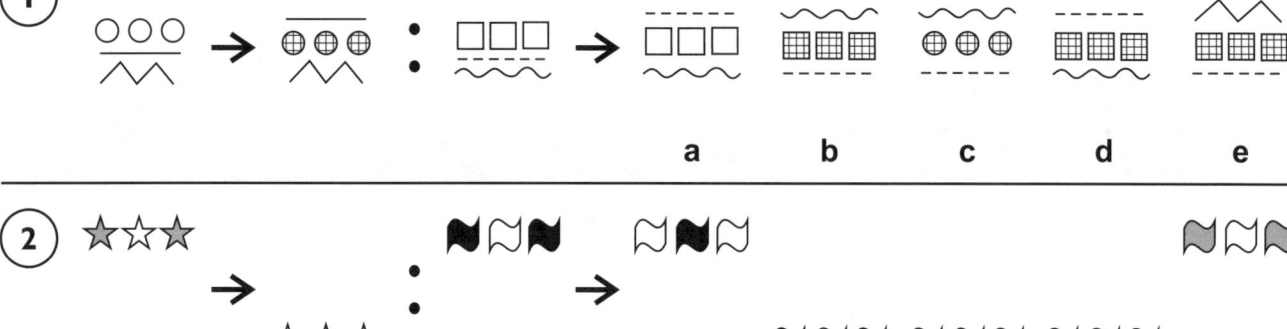

2.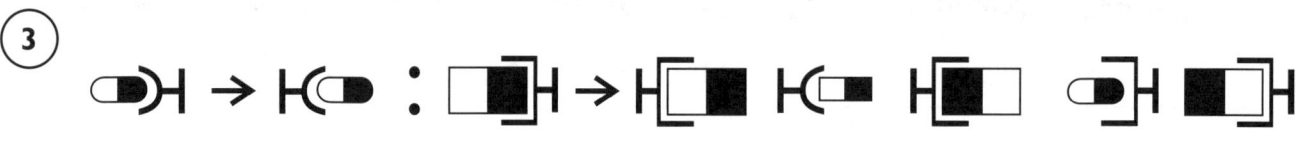

3.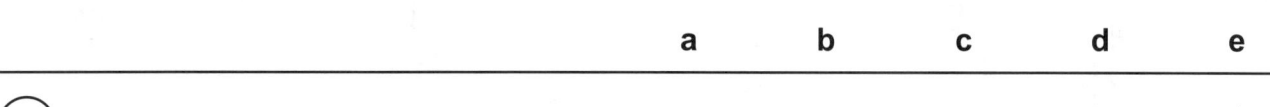

4.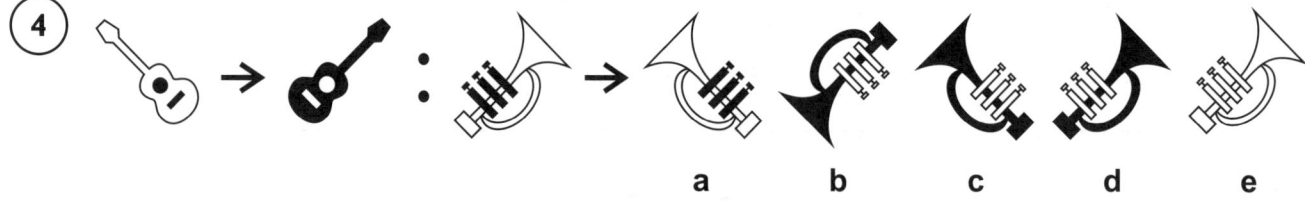

5.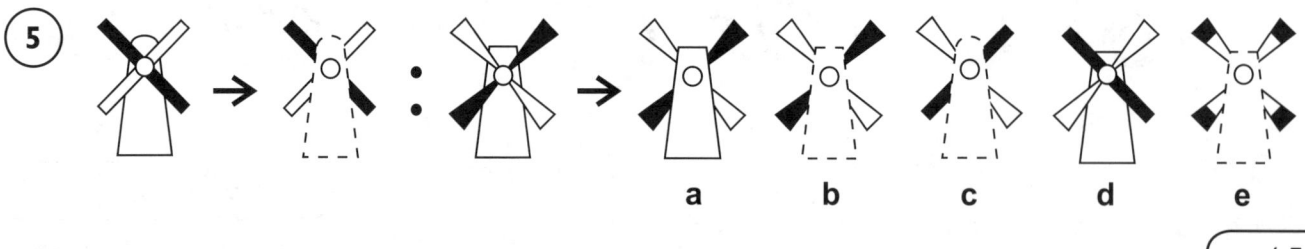

/ 5

Section 2 — Vertical Code

Each question has three figures on the left with code letters that describe them. You need to work out what the code letters mean. The figure on the right is missing its code. Work out which of the five codes on the right describes this figure.

Example:

→	P					
↑	Q	→	P	Q	T	S	R
←	R		a	b	c	d	e

Answer: a

The arrow pointing right has the code letter P. The arrow pointing up has the code letter Q. The arrow pointing left has the code letter R. The figure on the right is an arrow pointing right, so its code must be P and the answer is **a**.

---

1)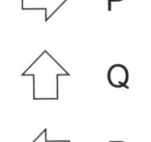

- BF
- CF
- CG

  BG   CG   CF   BE   BF
           a   b   c   d   e

---

2)

- XP
- YP
- ZQ

 YQ   ZP   XQ   XP   YP
           a   b   c   d   e

---

3)

- LR
- NS
- MR

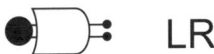 LS   MS   MR   NR   NS
           a   b   c   d   e

---

4)

- PT
- RS
- RT

 RS   PT   PR   PS   RT
           a   b   c   d   e

/ 4

Carry on to the next question → →

Assessment Test 8

Section 3 — Complete the Series

Each of these questions has five squares on the left that are arranged in order. One of the squares is empty. Work out which of the five squares on the right should replace the empty square.

Example: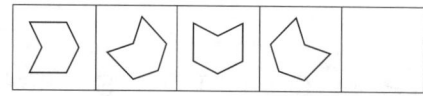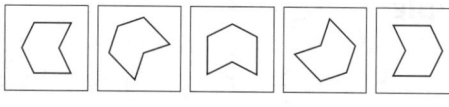

Answer: a

(1)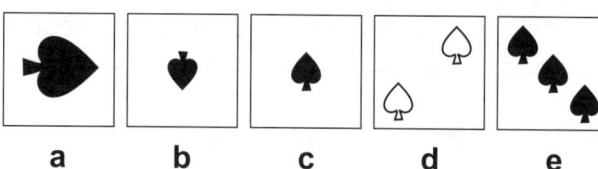

(2)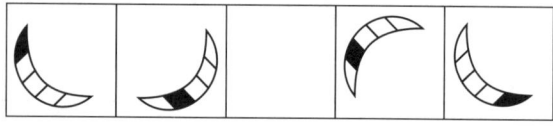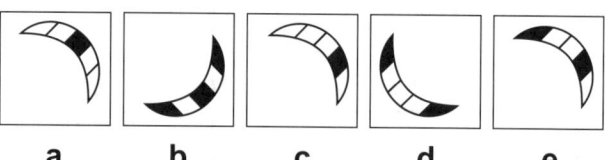

(3)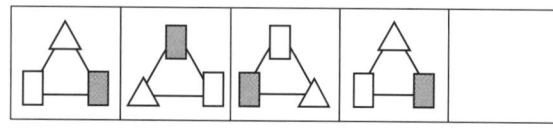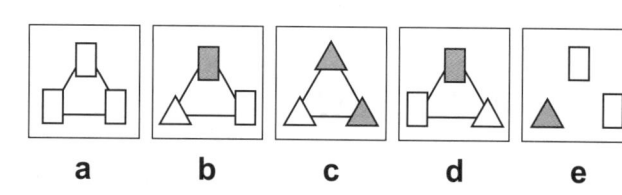

(4)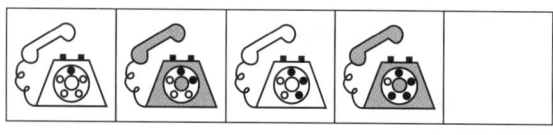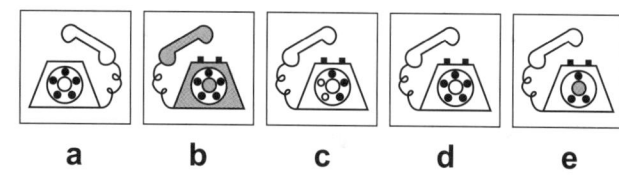

(5)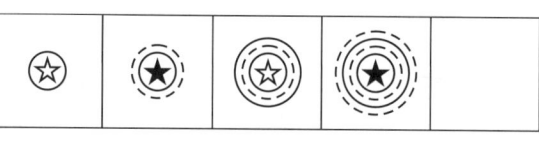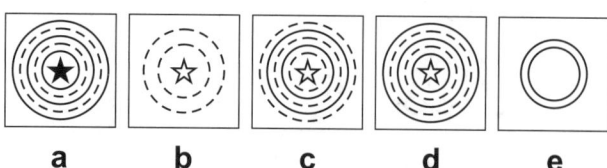

Assessment Test 8

Section 4 — Complete the Grid

On the left of each question below is a grid with one empty square.
Work out which of the five squares on the right should replace the empty square.

Example:

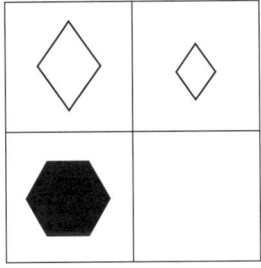 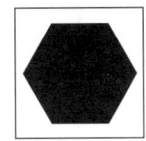   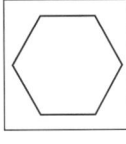 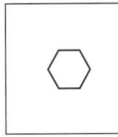

a   b   c   d   e

Answer: c

 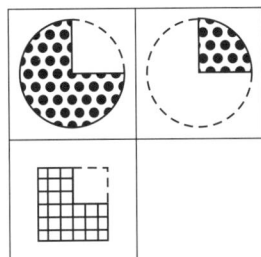 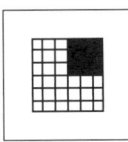 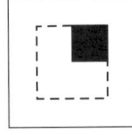 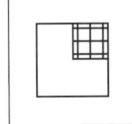 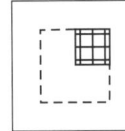 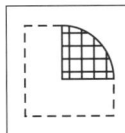

a   b   c   d   e

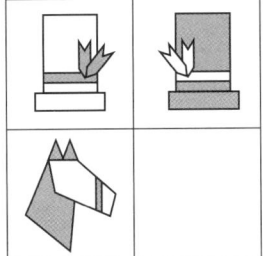 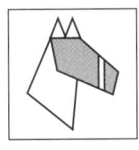 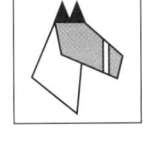 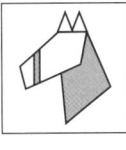 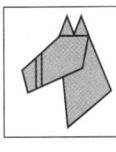 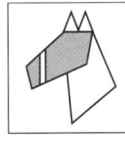

a   b   c   d   e

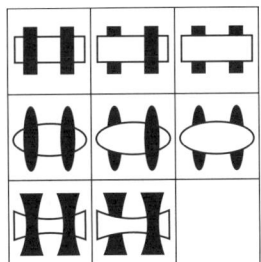  

a   b   c   d   e

  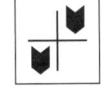 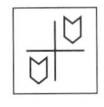 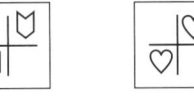

a   b   c   d   e   / 4

Carry on to the next question → →

Assessment Test 8

Section 5 — Find the Figure Like the First Three

In each question, there are three figures on the left that are like each other in some way. Work out which of the five figures on the right is most like the three figures on the left.

Example:

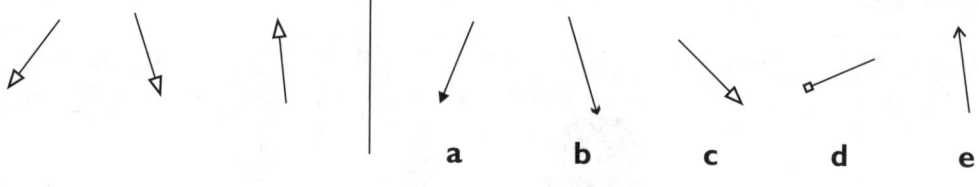

Answer: c

1)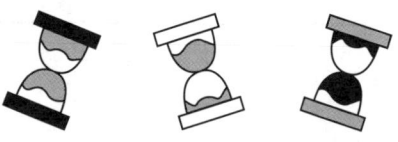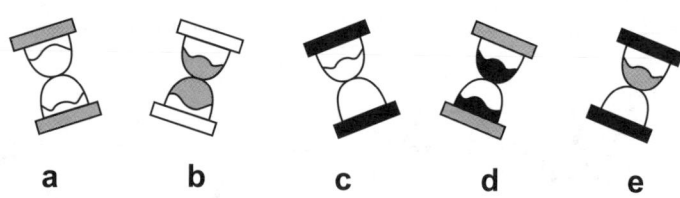

2)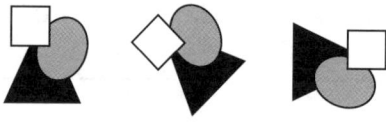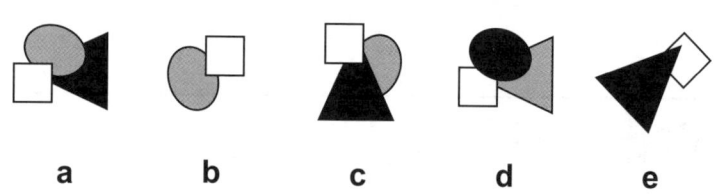

3)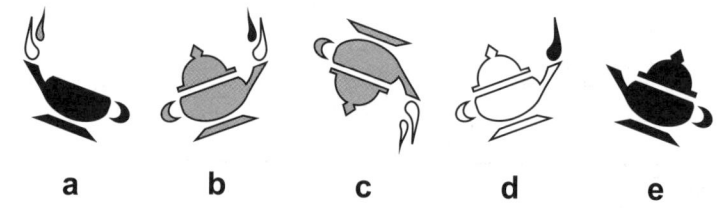

4)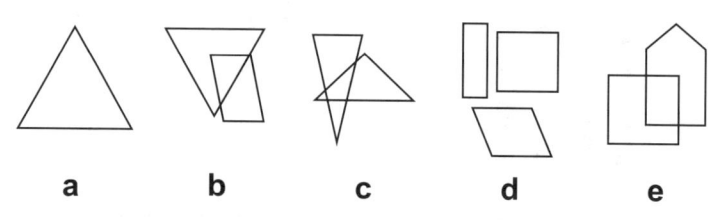

5)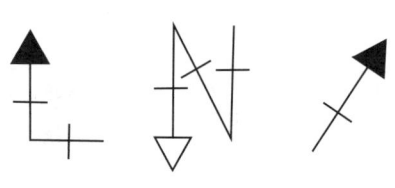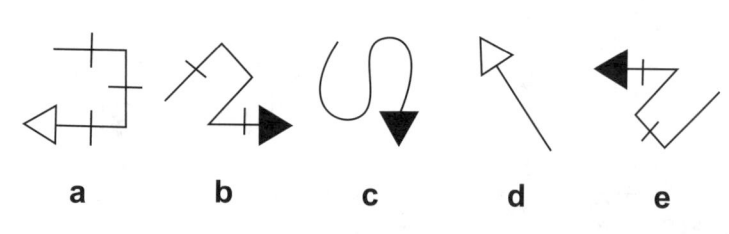

/ 5

Assessment Test 8

Section 6 — Odd One Out

Each of the questions below has five figures.
Find the figure in each row that is most unlike the others.

Example:

 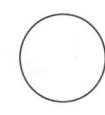   
a b c d e

Answer: b

1

 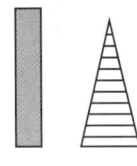 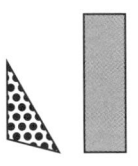 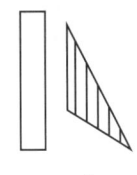 
a b c d e

2

  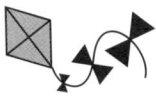 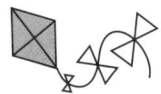 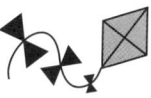
a b c d e

3

a b c d e

4

 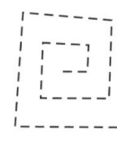 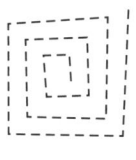  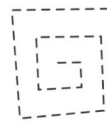
a b c d e

5

 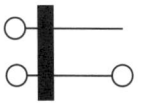
a b c d e

/ 5 Total / 28

End of Test

Assessment Test 8

Assessment Test 9

You can print **multiple-choice answer sheets** for these questions from our website — go to cgpbooks.co.uk/11plus/answer-sheets or scan the QR code on the right. If you'd prefer to answer them in standard write-in format, just circle the letter underneath your answer. The test should take around 15 minutes.

Section 1 — Find the Figure Like the First Two

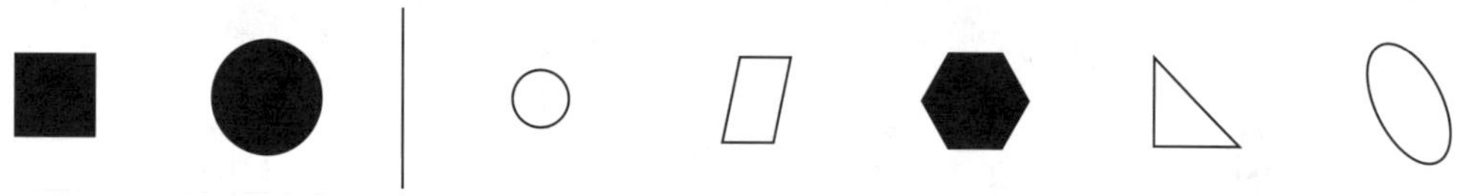

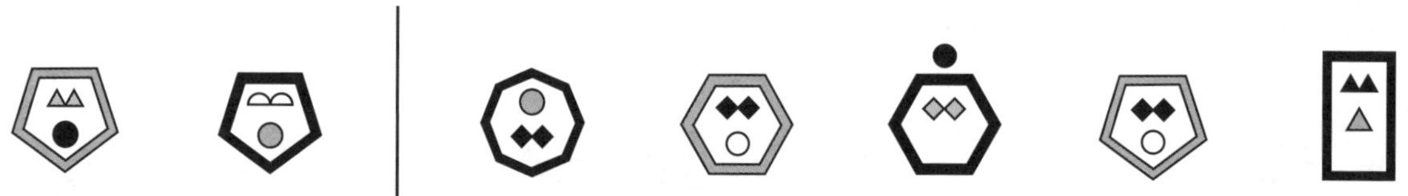

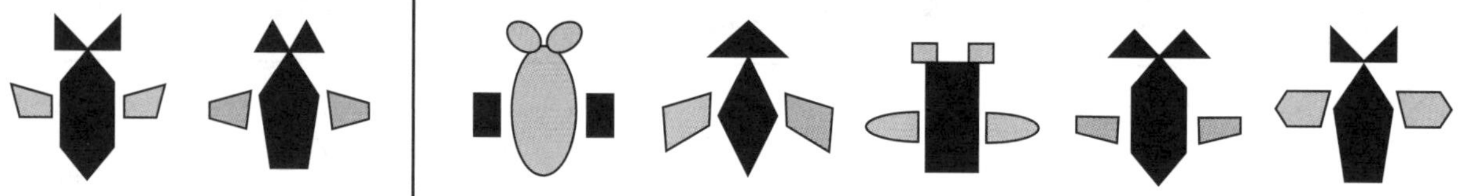

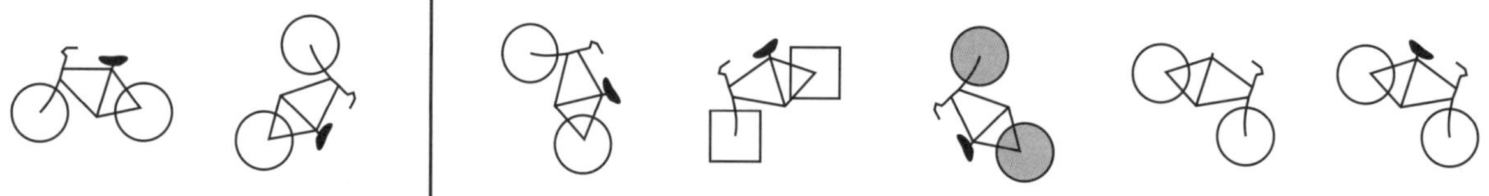

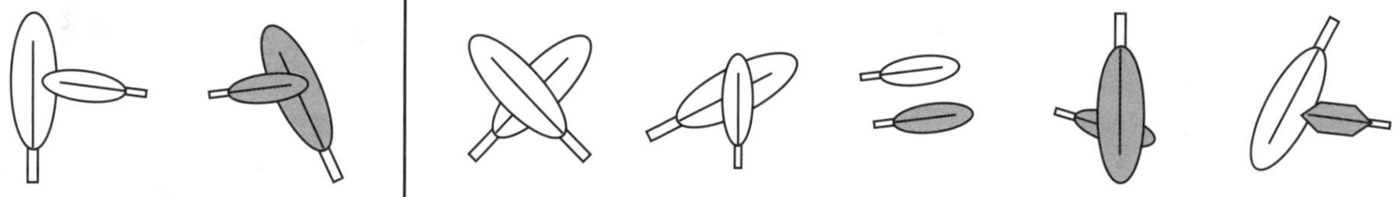

Section 2 — Odd One Out

Each of the questions below has five figures.
Find the figure in each row that is most unlike the others.

Example:

 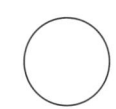   

a   b   c   d   e

Answer: b

1

  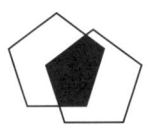  

a   b   c   d   e

2

    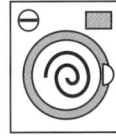

a   b   c   d   e

3

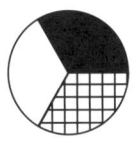 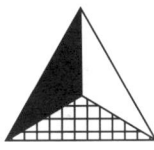 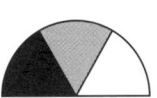 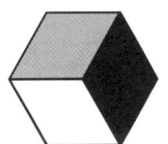 

a   b   c   d   e

4

 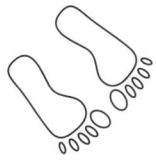 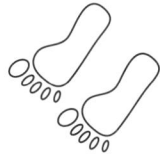 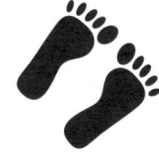 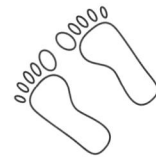

a   b   c   d   e

5

a   b   c   d   e

/ 5

Carry on to the next question → →

Assessment Test 9

Section 3 — Complete the Series

Each of these questions has five squares on the left that are arranged in order. One of the squares is empty. Work out which of the five squares on the right should replace the empty square.

Example: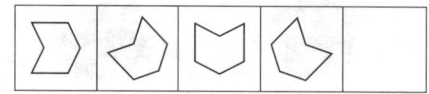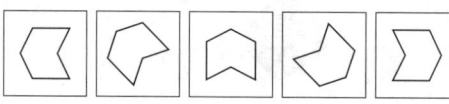

Answer: a

1
a b c d e

2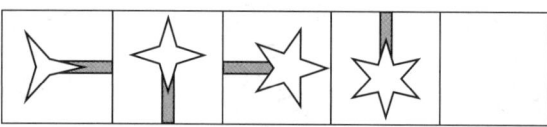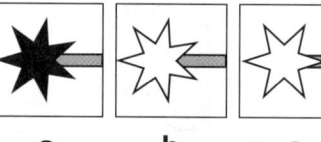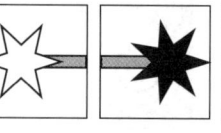
a b c d e

3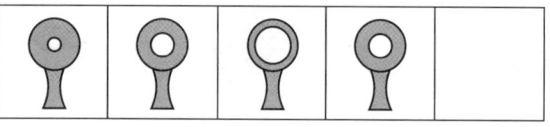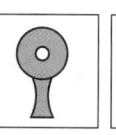
a b c d e

4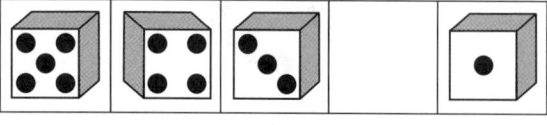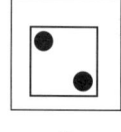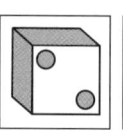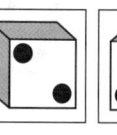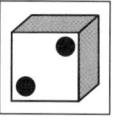
a b c d e

5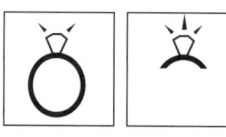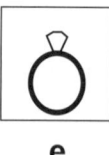
a b c d e

/ 5

Assessment Test 9

Section 4 — Complete the Pair

The first figure in each question changes to become the second figure. Work out how the first figure has been changed. Then find the figure on the right that would match the third figure if it was changed in the same way.

Example:

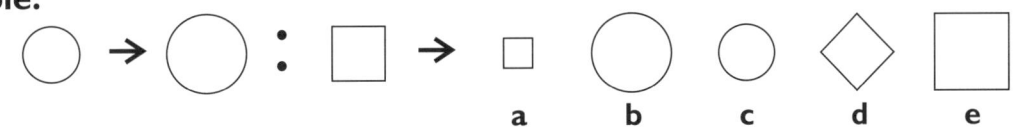

Answer: e

(1)  :

                                                      a   b   c   d   e

(2) 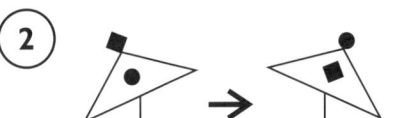 :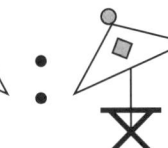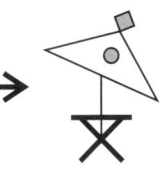

                                                      a   b   c   d   e

(3) 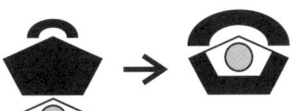 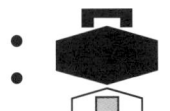 :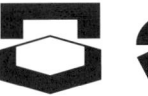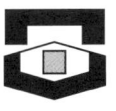

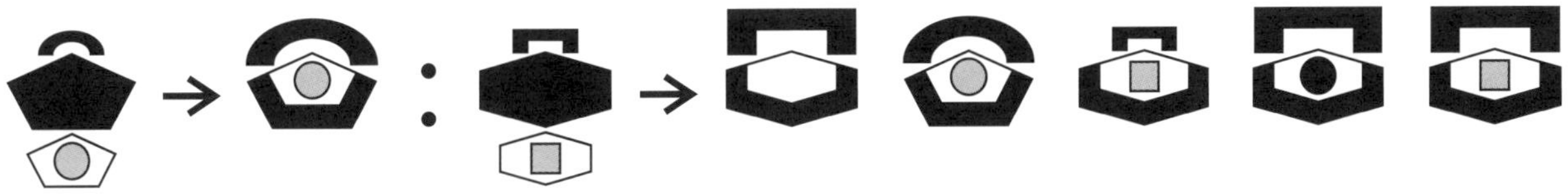

                                                      a   b   c   d   e

(4) 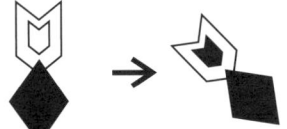 :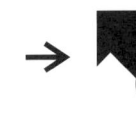

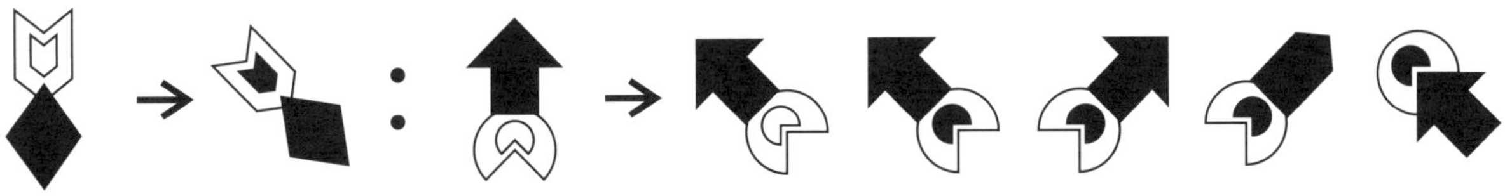

                                                      a   b   c   d   e

(5)   :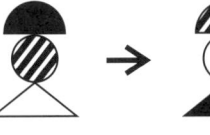

                                                      a   b   c   d   e

/ 5

Carry on to the next question → →

Section 5 — Vertical Code

Each question has three figures on the left with code letters that describe them. You need to work out what the code letters mean. The figure on the right is missing its code. Work out which of the five codes on the right describes this figure.

Example:

	P	Q	T	S	R
	a	b	c	d	e

Answer: a

The arrow pointing right has the code letter P. The arrow pointing up has the code letter Q. The arrow pointing left has the code letter R. The figure on the right is an arrow pointing right, so its code must be P and the answer is **a**.

1   GP
 FQ 
 GQ 

GR	FP	FQ	GQ	GP
a	b	c	d	e

2  JX
 LY 
 KX 

KY	LX	LY	JX	JY
a	b	c	d	e

3   SM
 TM
 UN 

TN	UM	TM	SN	UN
a	b	c	d	e

4   VF
 VG 
 WH 

VG	VF	WF	VH	WG
a	b	c	d	e

Section 6 — Complete the Grid

On the left of each question below is a grid with one empty square.
Work out which of the five squares on the right should replace the empty square.

Example:

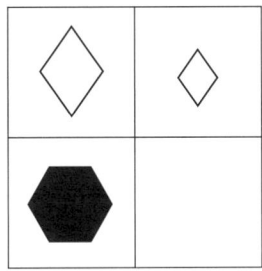   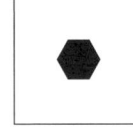 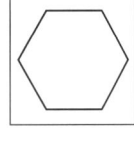 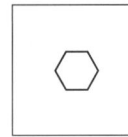

a b c d e

Answer: c

1)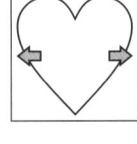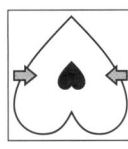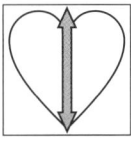

a b c d e

2)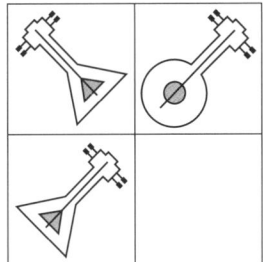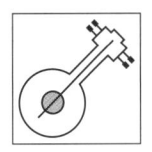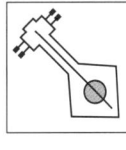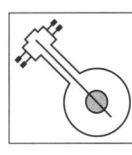

a b c d e

3)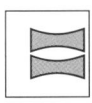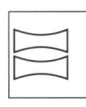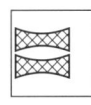

a b c d e

4)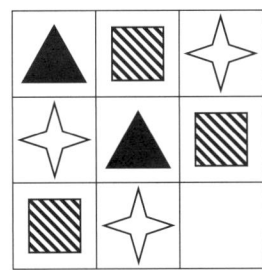

a b c d e

/ 4   Total / 28

End of Test

Assessment Test 9

Assessment Test 10

You can print **multiple-choice answer sheets** for these questions from our website — go to cgpbooks.co.uk/11plus/answer-sheets or scan the QR code on the right. If you'd prefer to answer them in standard write-in format, just circle the letter underneath your answer. The test should take around 15 minutes.

Section 1 — Complete the Series

Each of these questions has five squares on the left that are arranged in order. One of the squares is empty. Work out which of the five squares on the right should replace the empty square.

Example: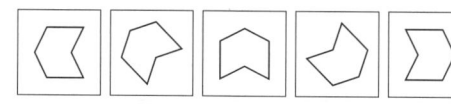

Answer: a

1)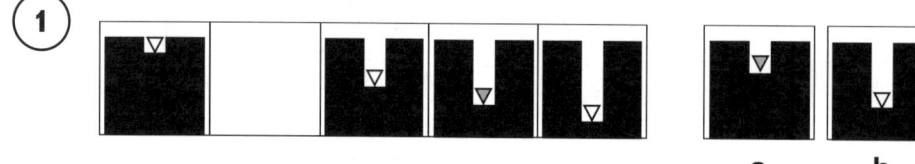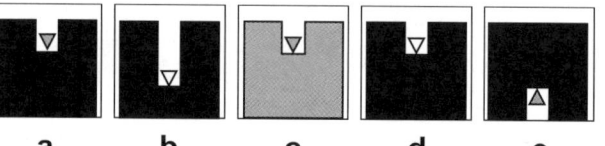

2)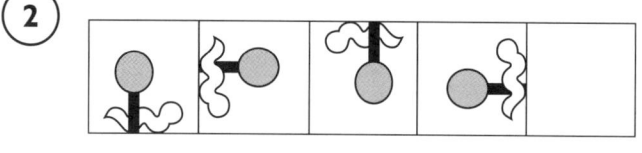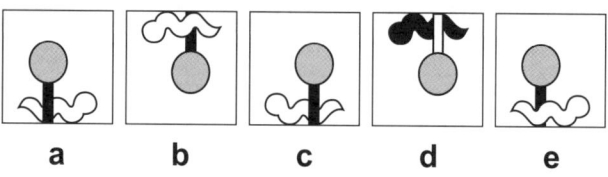

3)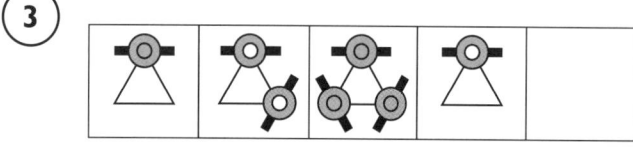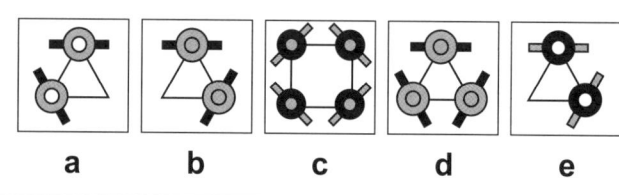

4)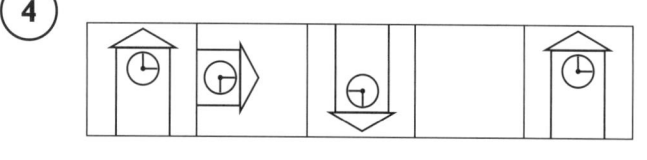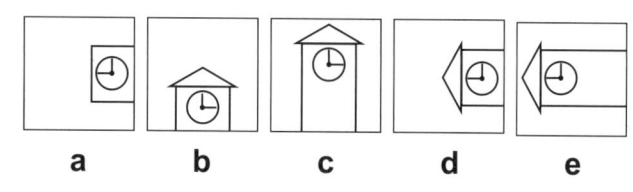

5)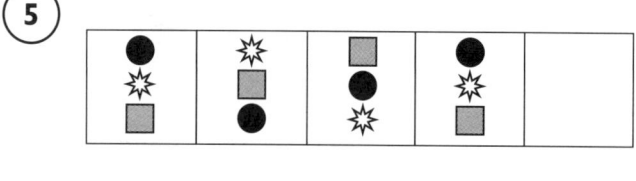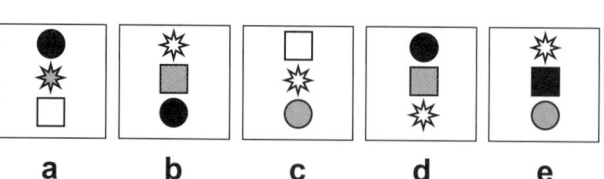

Section 2 — Complete the Grid

On the left of each question below is a grid with one empty square.
Work out which of the five squares on the right should replace the empty square.

Example:

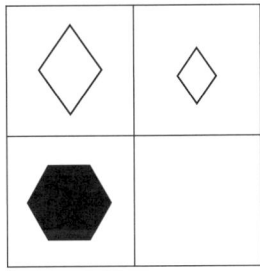 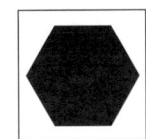 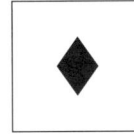 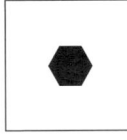 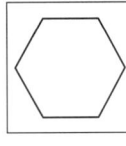 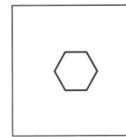

a   b   c   d   e

Answer: c

(1)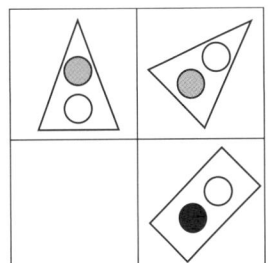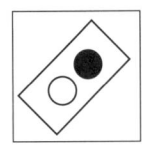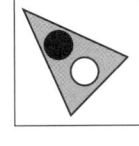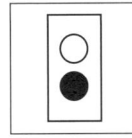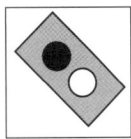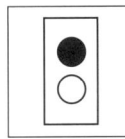

a   b   c   d   e

(2)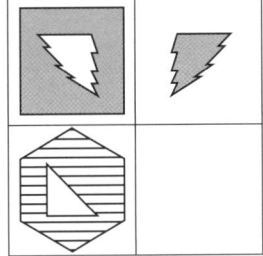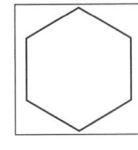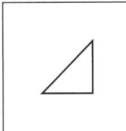

a   b   c   d   e

(3)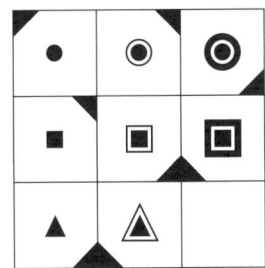

a   b   c   d   e

(4)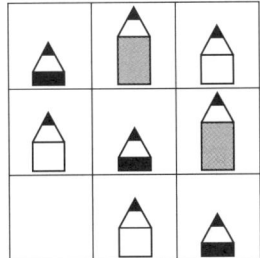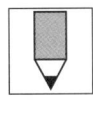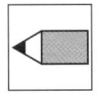

a   b   c   d   e

/ 4

Carry on to the next question →→

Assessment Test 10

Section 3 — Vertical Code

Each question has three figures on the left with code letters that describe them. You need to work out what the code letters mean. The figure on the right is missing its code. Work out which of the five codes on the right describes this figure.

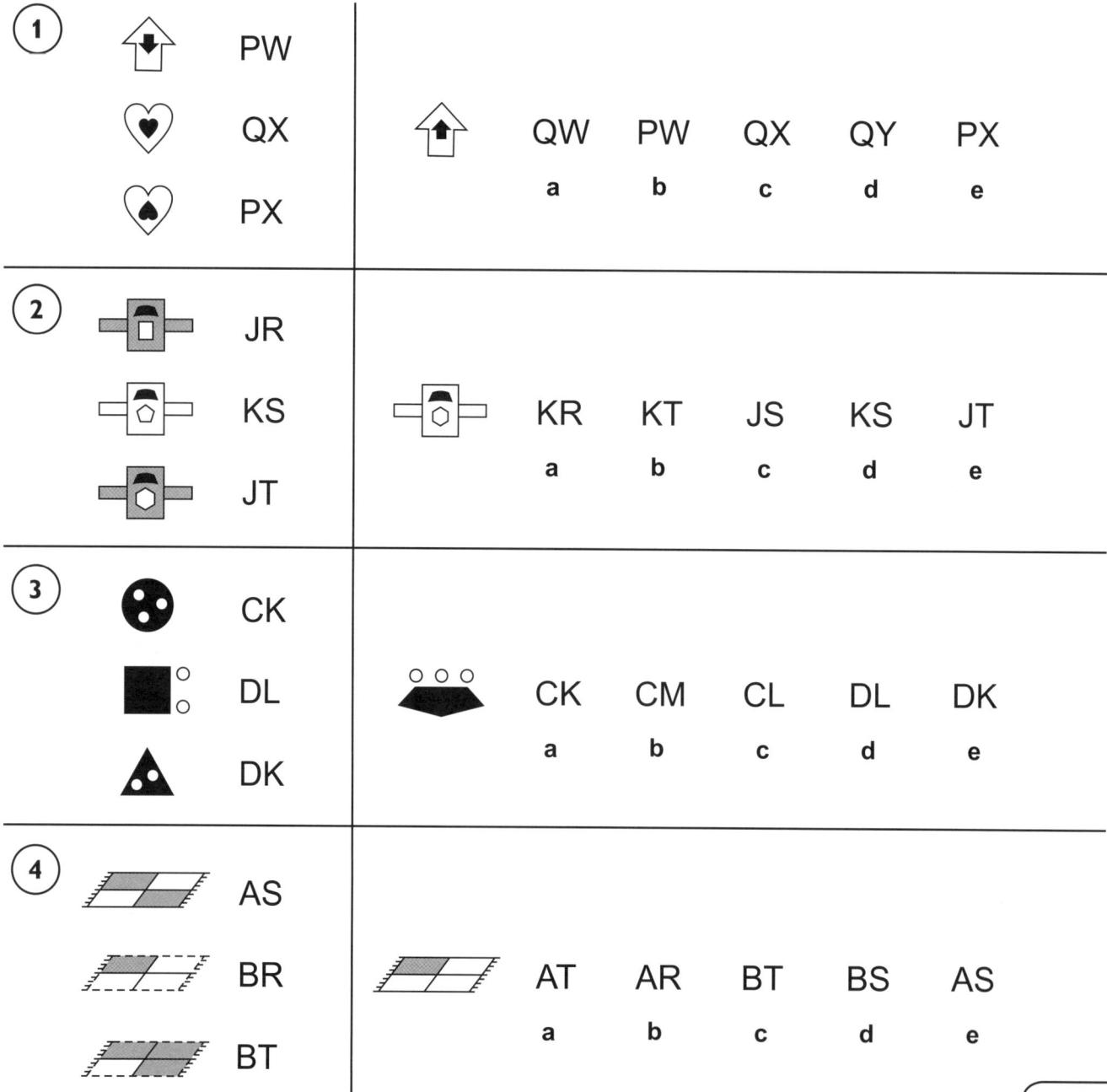

Section 4 — Find the Figure Like the First Three

In each question, there are three figures on the left that are like each other in some way. Work out which of the five figures on the right is most like the three figures on the left.

Example:

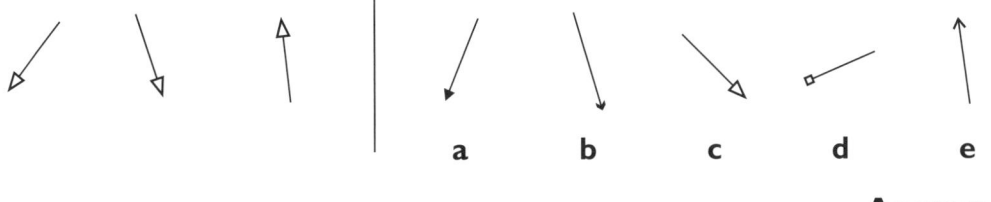

Answer: c

 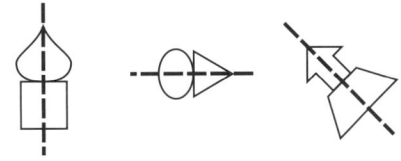 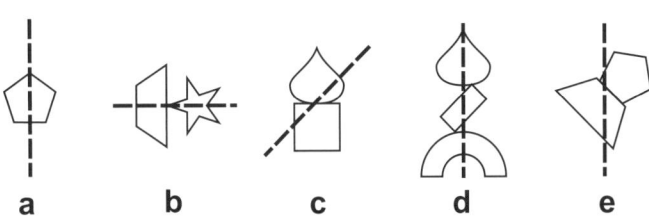

  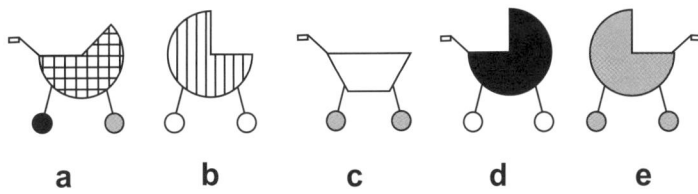

  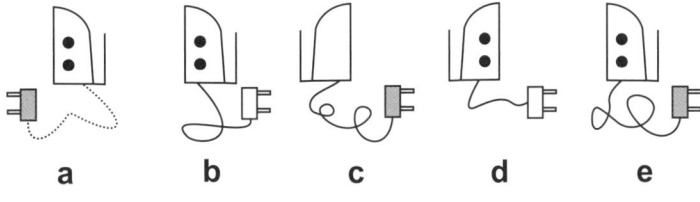

      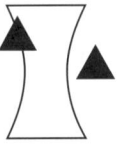 

/ 5

Carry on to the next question → →

Assessment Test 10

Section 5 — Odd One Out

Each of the questions below has five figures.
Find the figure in each row that is most unlike the others.

Example:

a　　　b　　　c　　　d　　　e

Answer: b

1

a　　　b　　　c　　　d　　　e

2

a　　　b　　　c　　　d　　　e

3

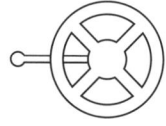　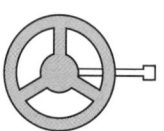　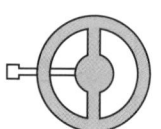　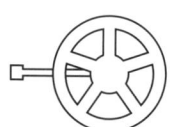　

a　　　b　　　c　　　d　　　e

4

a　　　b　　　c　　　d　　　e

5

　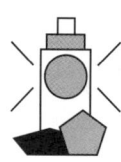　　　

a　　　b　　　c　　　d　　　e

/ 5

Assessment Test 10

Section 6 — Complete the Pair

The first figure in each question changes to become the second figure. Work out how the first figure has been changed. Then find the figure on the right that would match the third figure if it was changed in the same way.

Example:

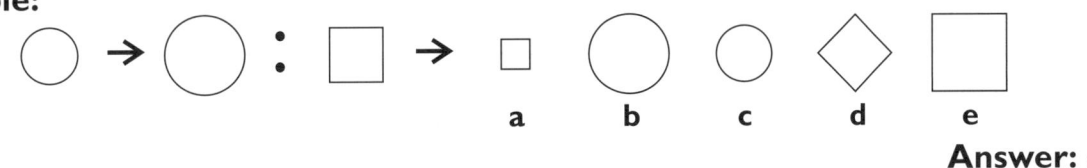

Answer: e

1.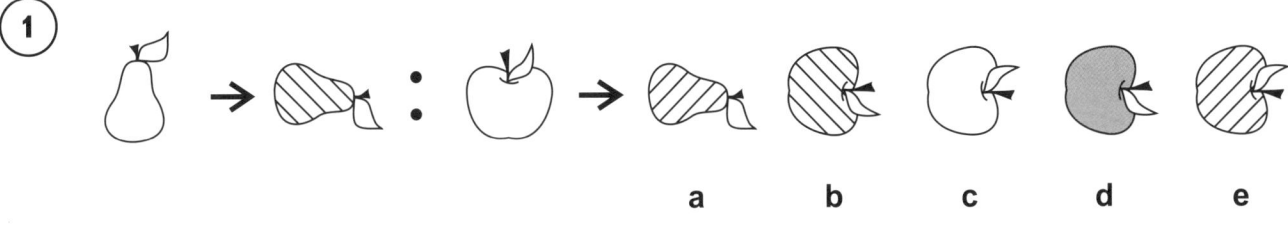

2.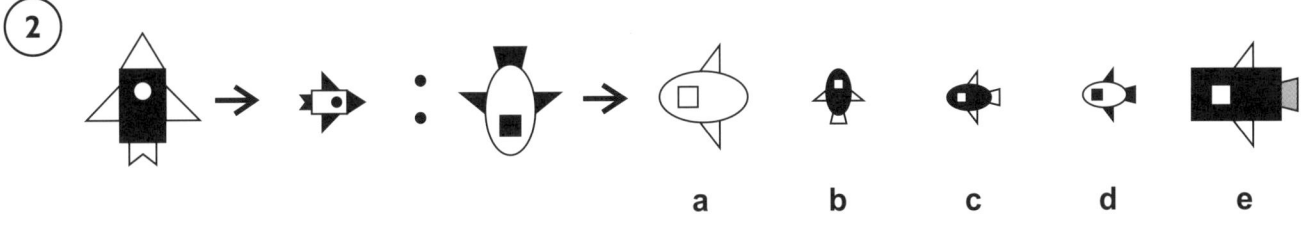

3.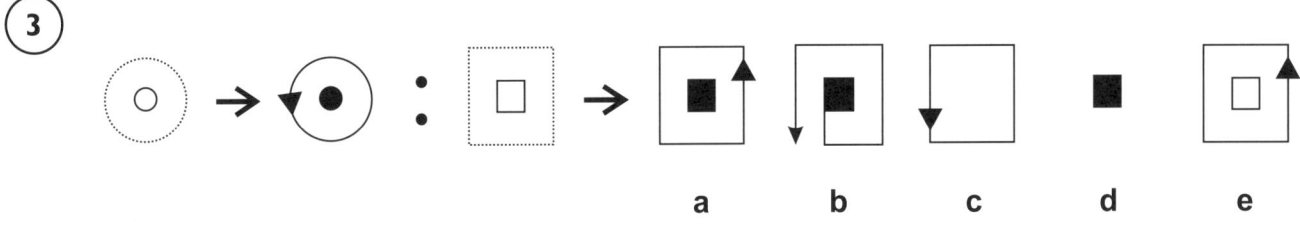

4.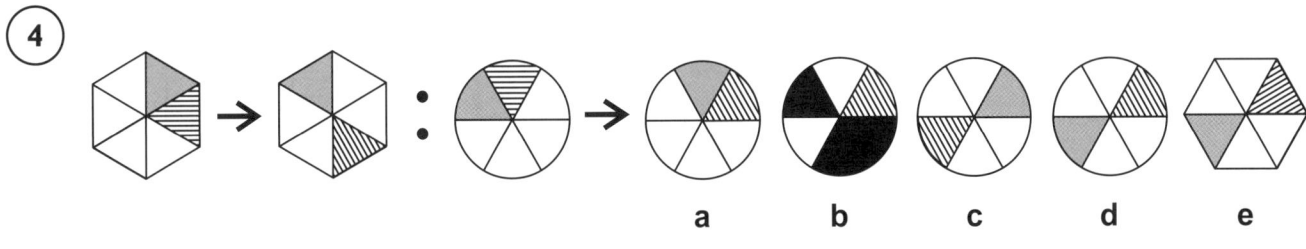

5.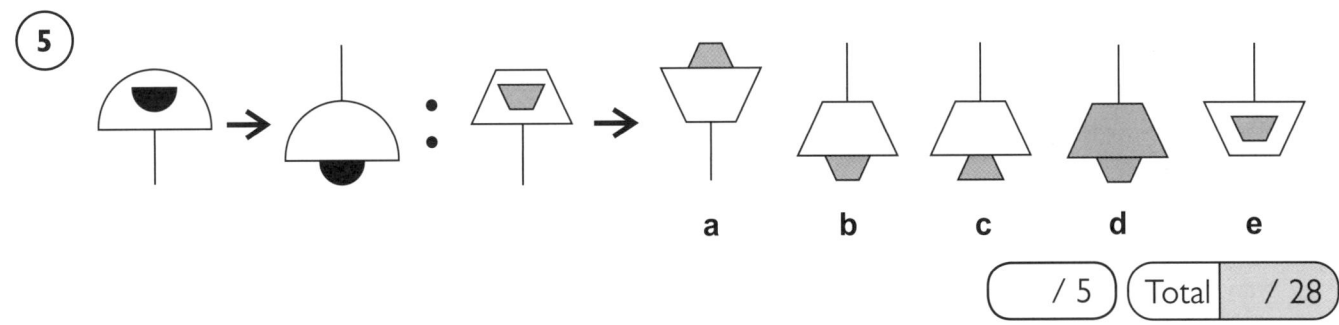

/ 5   Total / 28

End of Test

Assessment Test 10

Assessment Test 11

You can print **multiple-choice answer sheets** for these questions from our website — go to cgpbooks.co.uk/11plus/answer-sheets or scan the QR code on the right. If you'd prefer to answer them in standard write-in format, just circle the letter underneath your answer. The test should take around 15 minutes.

You can ignore Test 11 if you're sitting the test in a region that doesn't test Spatial Reasoning. For more information on test content in different regions, please visit cgpbooks.co.uk/11plus.

Section 1 — Hidden Shape

Each of these questions has a single shape on the left. This shape can be found in one of the five figures on the right. The shape must be the same size and orientation. Find which of the five figures contains the shape.

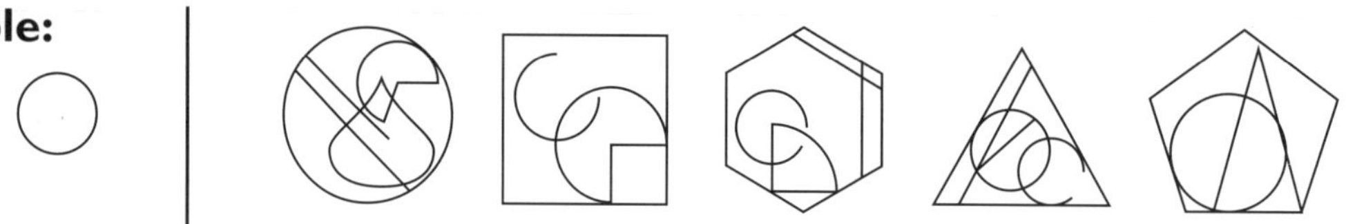

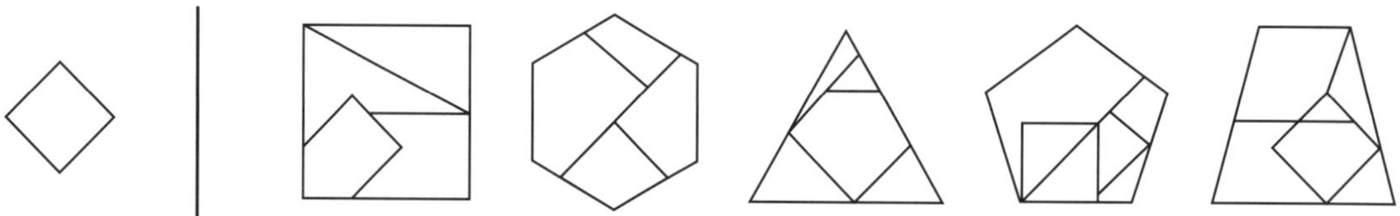

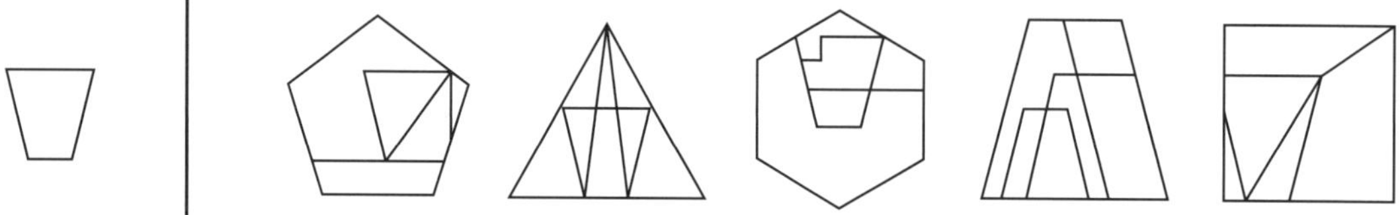

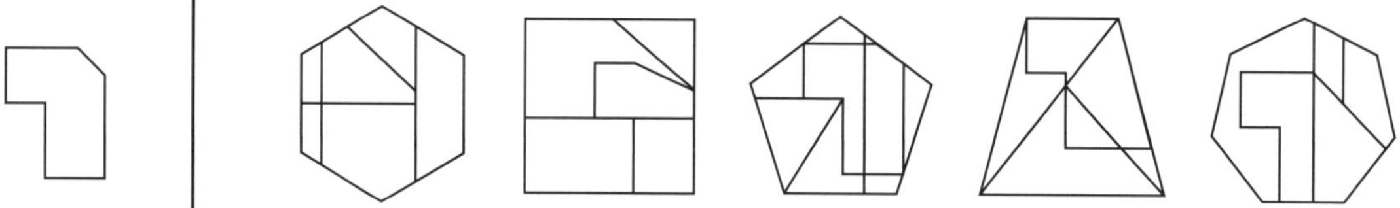

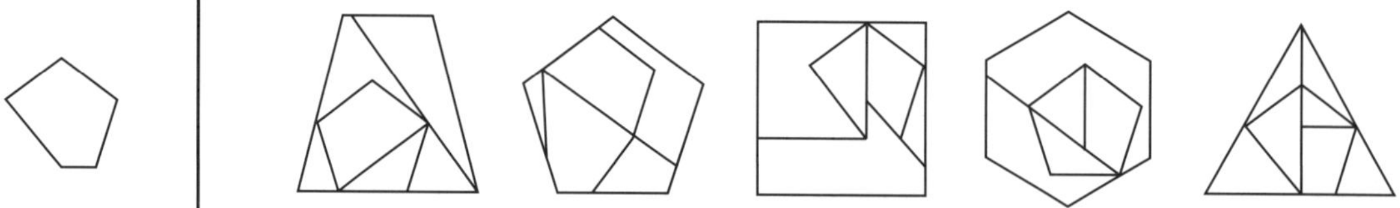

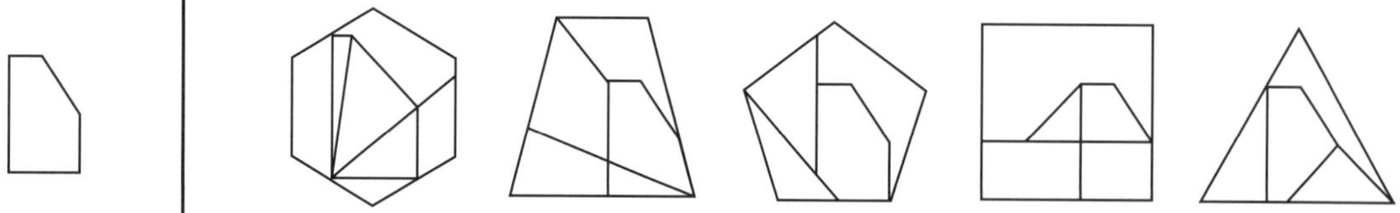

Section 2 — Look at the Figure from the Right

Each of these questions has a 3D figure on the left, made out of blocks. Work out which of the five options shows what the figure would look like if you saw it from the right-hand side.

Example:

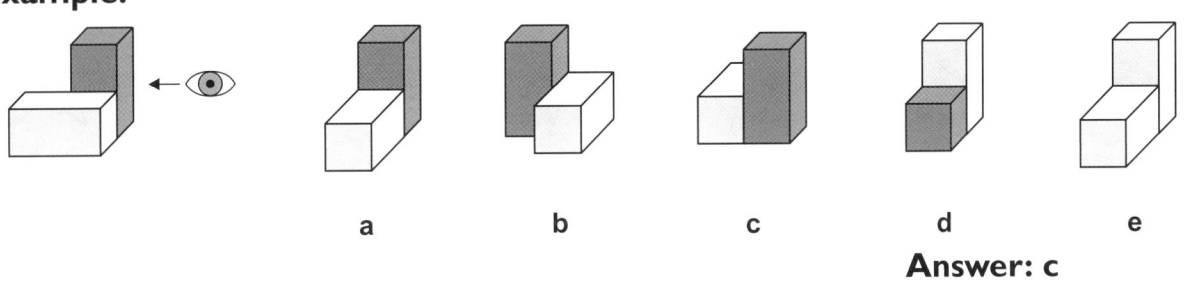

Answer: c

1

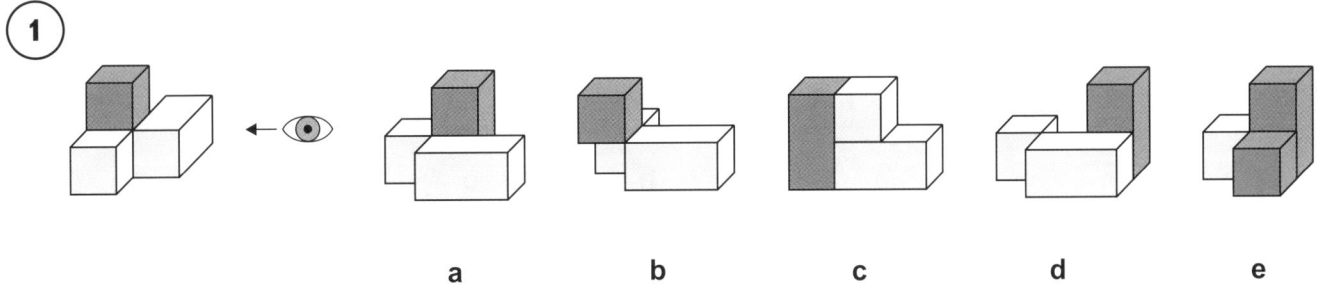

2

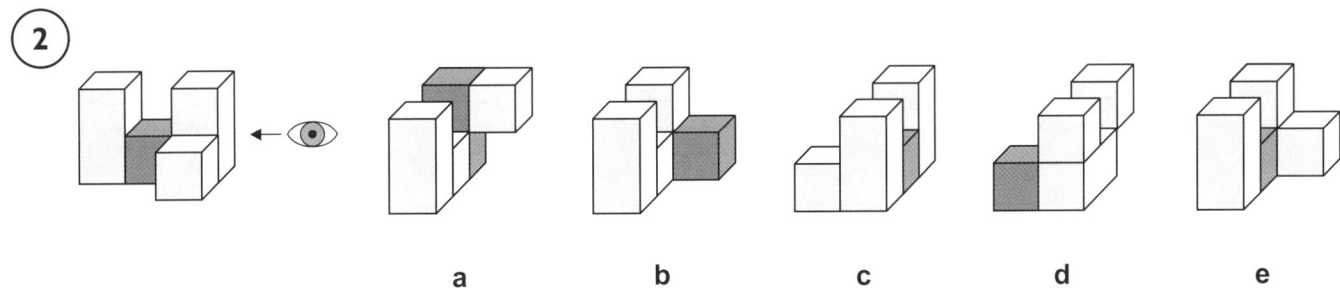

3

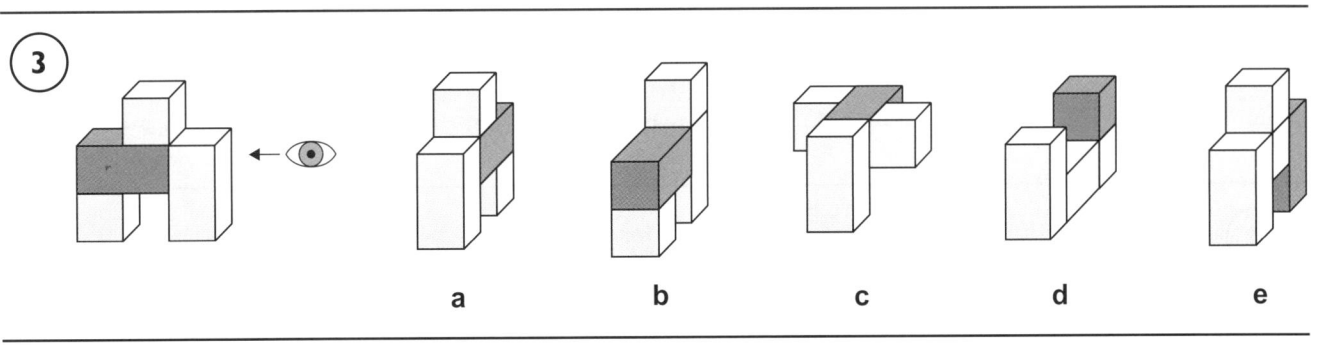

4

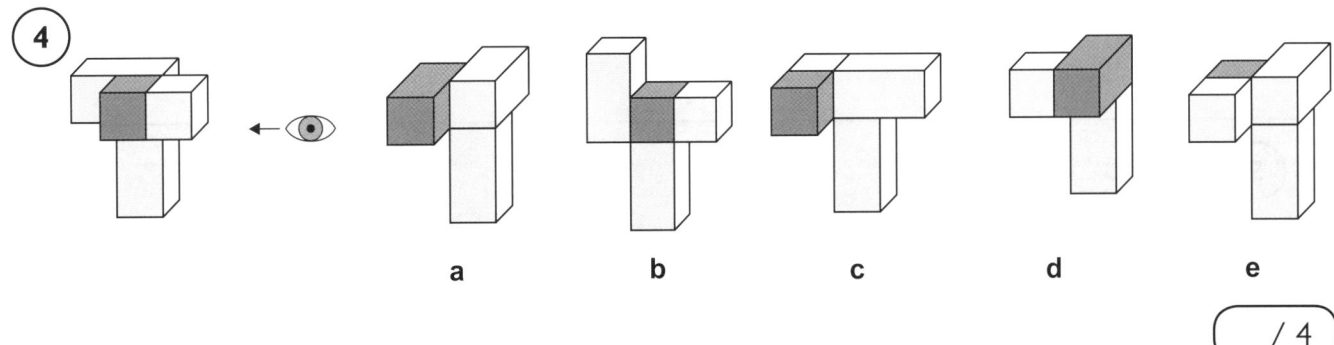

/ 4

Carry on to the next question → →

Section 3 — Fold Along the Line

Each question has a shape on the left with a dotted fold line.
This shape is followed by a choice of five shapes. Choose the shape that shows how the shape on the left would look if it was folded along the fold line.

Example:

 |
                                    a   b   c   d   e

Answer: b

1. 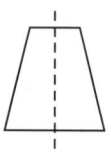 |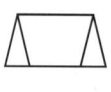
a   b   c   d   e

2. 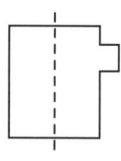 |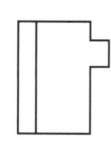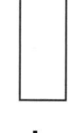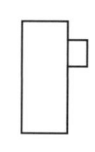
a   b   c   d   e

3. 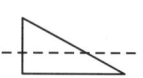 |
a   b   c   d   e

4. 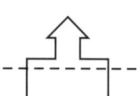 |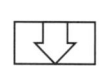
a   b   c   d   e

5. 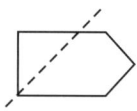 |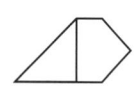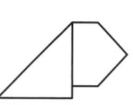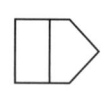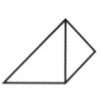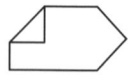
a   b   c   d   e

/ 5

Assessment Test 11

Section 4 — Look at the Figure from the Top

Each of these questions has a 3D figure on the left, made out of cubes.
Work out which of the five options is a top-down 2D view of the 3D figure on the left.

Example:

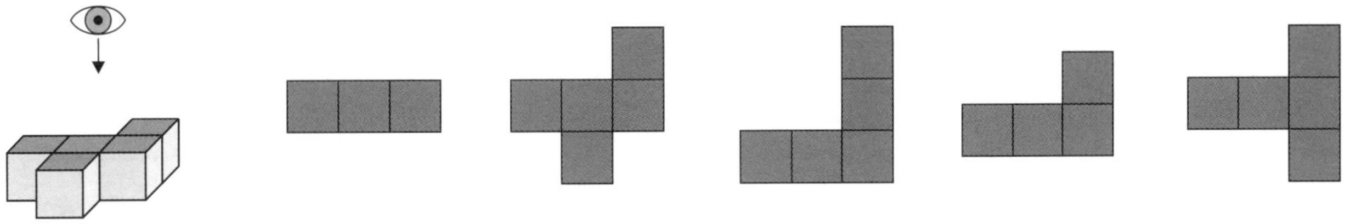

a b c d e

Answer: b

1)

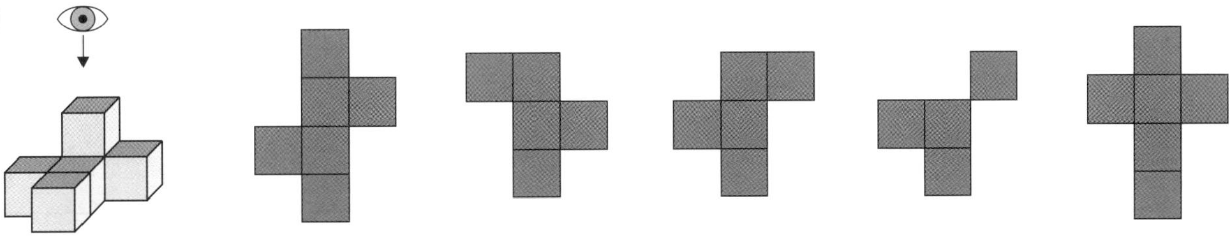

a b c d e

2)

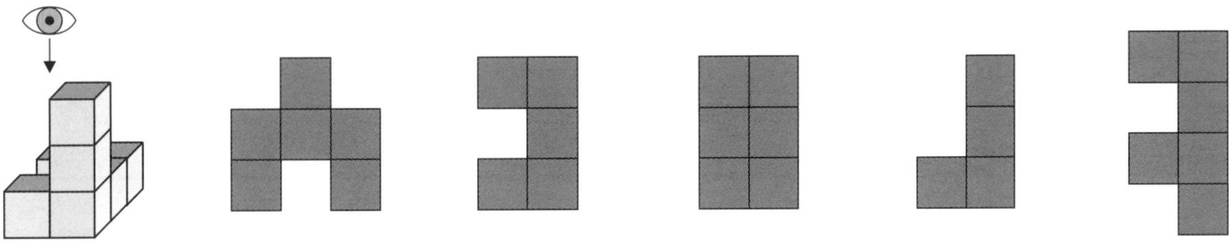

a b c d e

3)

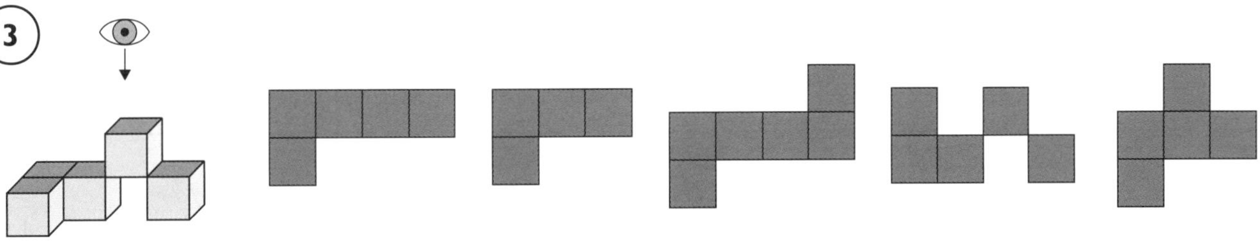

a b c d e

4)

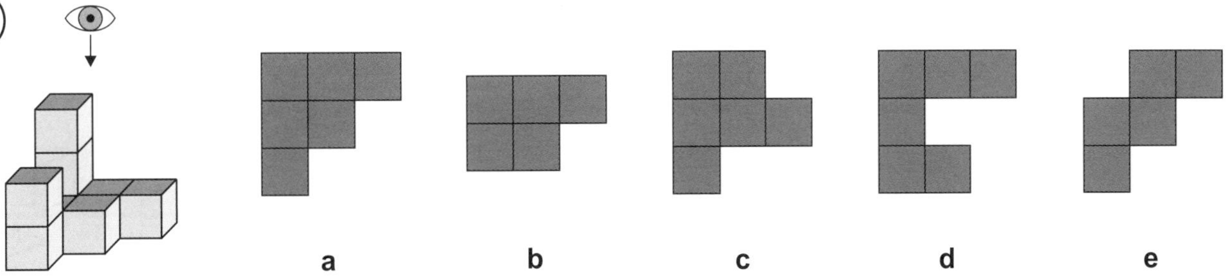

a b c d e

/ 4

Carry on to the next question → →

Assessment Test 11

Section 5 — Connecting Shapes

Each of these questions has three shapes on the left. Some of their sides are labelled with a letter. Choose the option which shows how the shapes would look if they were joined together so that sides with the same letter are touching.

Example:

Answer: e

1

2

3

4

5

/ 5

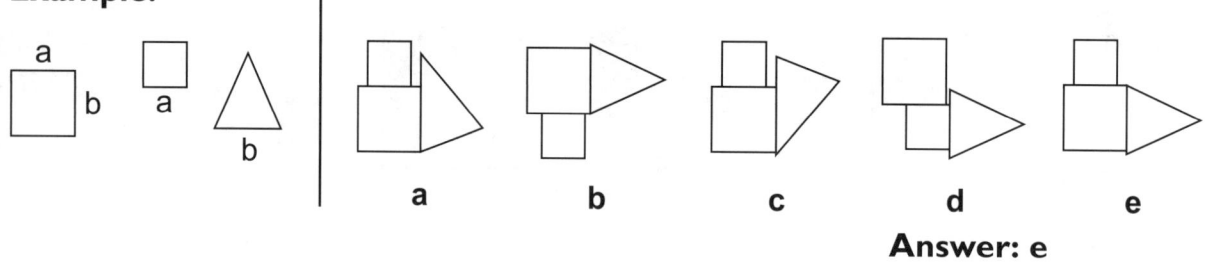

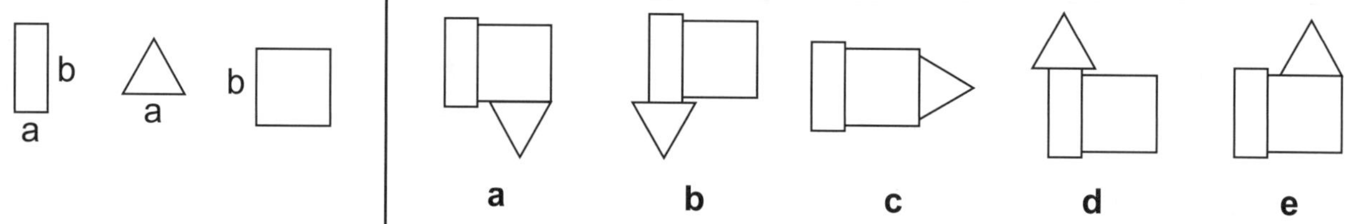

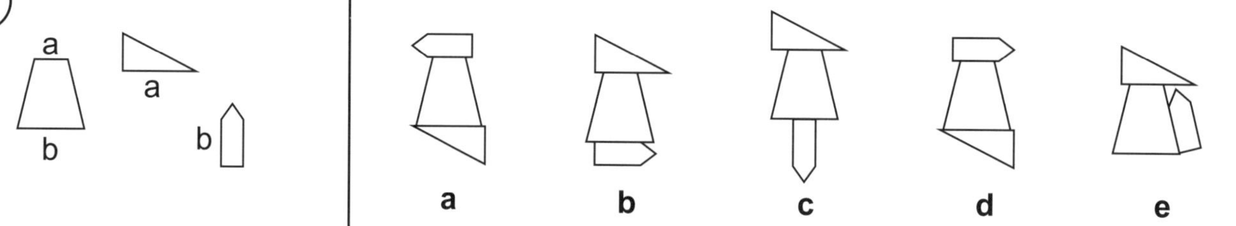

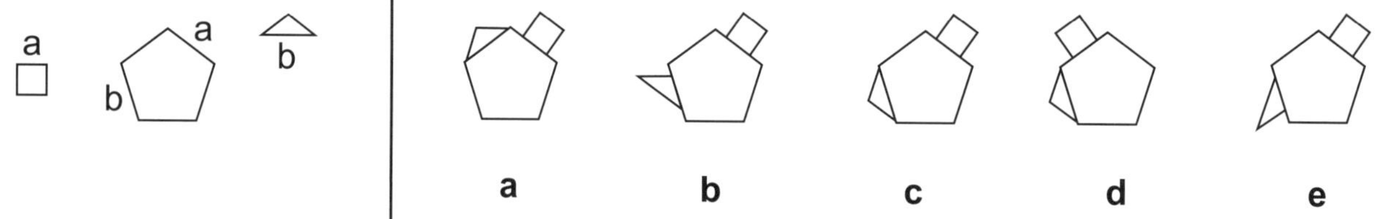

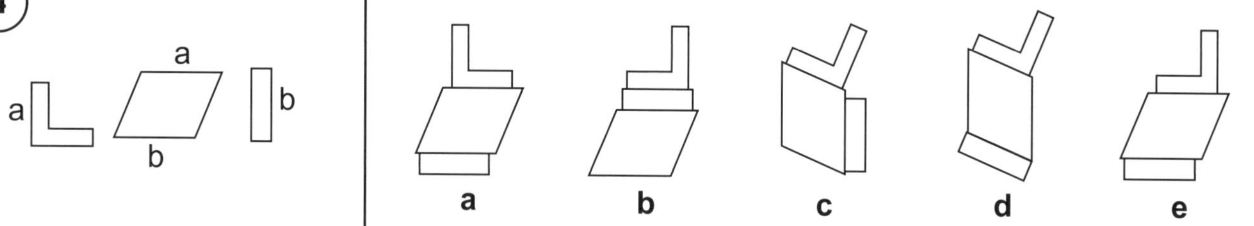

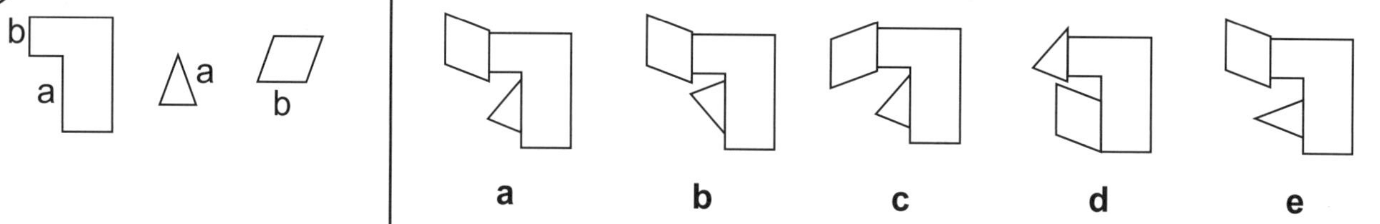

Section 6 — Fold and Punch

Each of these questions shows a square of paper being folded several times. A hole is then punched in the folded piece of paper. Work out which of the five options shows what the piece of paper would look like if it was unfolded.

Example:

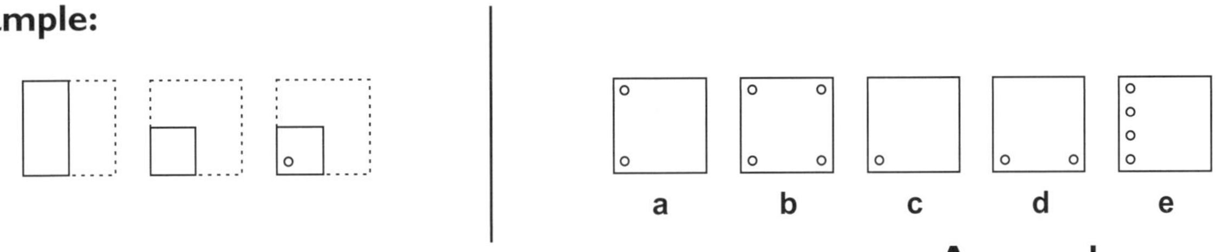

Answer: b

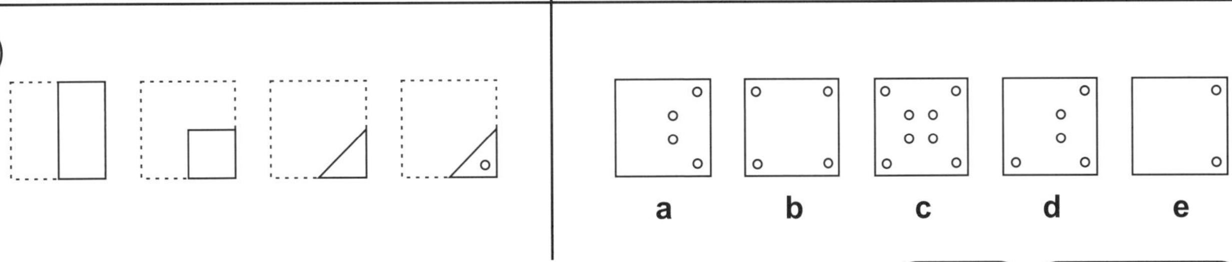

/ 5   Total / 28

End of Test

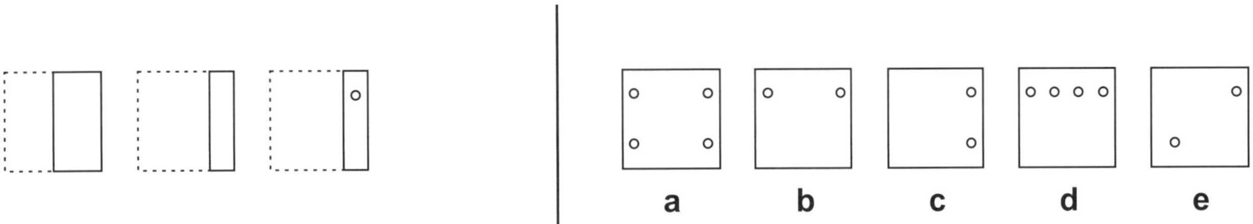

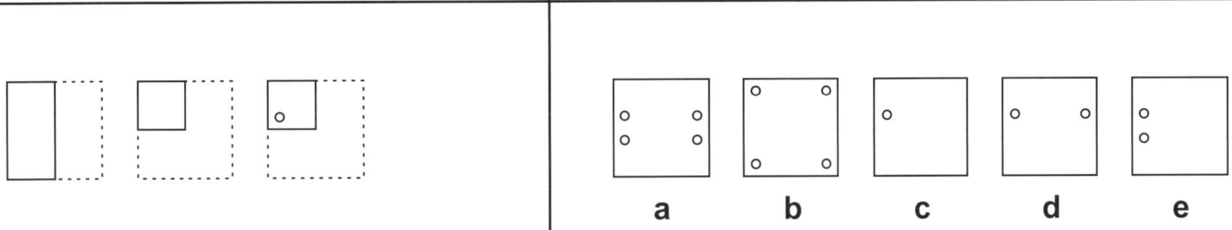

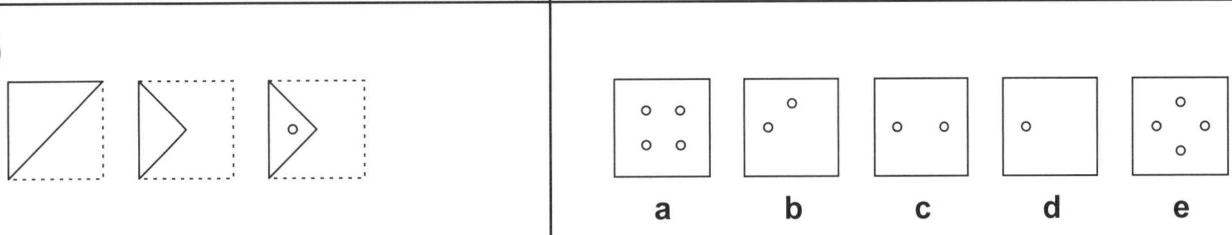

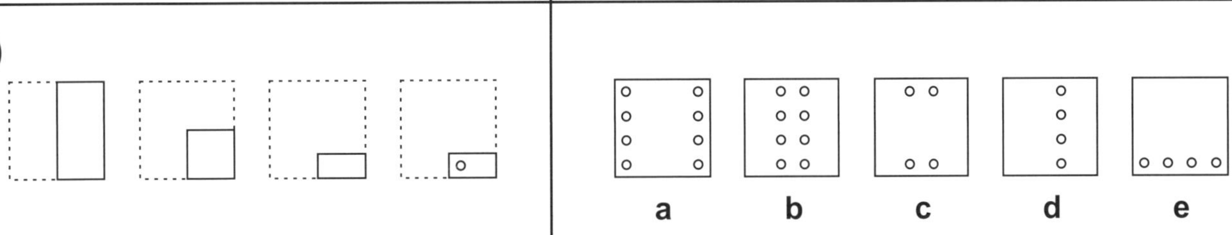

Assessment Test 11

Glossary

Rotation

Rotation is when a shape is **turned** clockwise or anticlockwise.

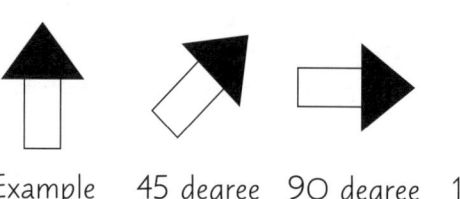

Example shape | 45 degree rotation | 90 degree rotation | 180 degree rotation

Clockwise is the direction that the hands on a clock move

Anticlockwise is the opposite direction

Reflection

Reflection is when something is **mirrored** over a line (this line might be invisible).

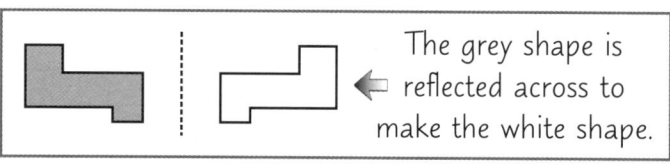

The grey shape is reflected across to make the white shape.

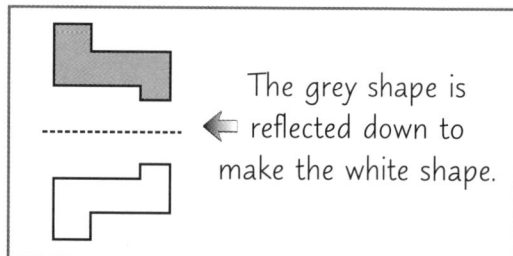

The grey shape is reflected down to make the white shape.

Other terms

Figure — the picture as a whole that makes up one example or option in a question.

Line Types:

Thin | Thick | Dashed | Dotted | Curved | Jagged | Wavy

Shading Types:

Black | Grey | White | Two types of hatching | Cross-hatched | Spotted

Layering — when a shape is in front of or behind another shape, or when shapes overlap each other.

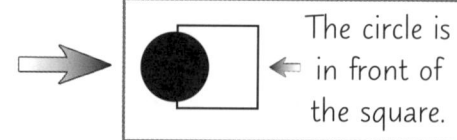

The circle is in front of the square.

Symmetry — a shape is symmetrical if it can be split into halves that are reflections of each other.

Glossary

Answers

Spotting Patterns

Pages 2-3 — Shapes

Warm Up

1) a) 5   b) 7   c) 7   d) 6   e) 8   f) 5

2) Number of same-sided grey shapes: 2 (the second and fourth figures both have a grey shape with seven sides).

Find the Figure Like the First Two

3) D
In all figures, the large white shape must have four sides.

4) C
All figures must have two identical shapes that overlap.

5) D
In all figures, there must be two separate shapes — a large shape and a small shape. Both shapes must be shaded differently to each other. The small shape must be the same size as a third of the large shape.

Vertical Code

6) E (X)
X = five-sided black shape, Y = four-sided black shape, Z = six-sided black shape.

7) E (GL)
F = a white hexagon, G = a white pentagon.
L = a wide grey ellipse, M = a grey circle.

8) B (CQ)
B = medium-length wavy lines, C = short wavy lines, D = long wavy lines.
P = a hatched parallelogram, Q = a hatched rectangle.

Pages 4-5 — Counting

Warm Up

1) a) 3   b) 3   c) 5   d) 4   e) 4   f) 7

2) Number of cakes with the same number of layers: 2 (the second and fourth cakes also have four layers).
Number of cakes with the same number of cherries: 1 (the first cake also has four cherries).

Complete the Series

3) B
The zebra gains an extra stripe in each series square.

4) E
The series alternates between two and three stars.
The stars gain an extra point in each series square.

5) D
The white shape gains an extra side in each series square.
An extra dot is added inside the white shape.

Find the Figure Like the First Three

6) A
All stars must have two black points.

7) B
All figures must have two black dots and four small inner lines.

8) E
All figures must be four-sided white shapes, with three inner lines that go from one side of the shape to another.

Page 6 — Pointing

Warm Up

1) a) square   b) triangle   c) star
   d) circle   e) square   f) triangle

2) Number of arrows that point in the same direction: 2 (the second and fourth figures both point diagonally down to the right).

Odd One Out

3) E
In all other figures, the arrow points away from the cannon.

4) D
In all other figures, the arrow points in a clockwise direction.

Page 7 — Shading and Line Types

Warm Up

1) a) grey   b) black   c) white
   d) black   e) grey   f) white

2) Number of paintings with the same direction of hatching: 1 (the third figure is the only figure which is hatched going diagonally down to the left).
Number of paintings with the same type of line: 3 (the first, second and fourth figures are the only figures with dotted hatched lines).

Odd One Out

3) B
In all other figures, the line between the circle and the black shape at the top is thick. (In B the line is thin.)

4) D
All other figures have three wavy lines. (D has three jagged lines.)

Pages 8-9 — Order and Position

Warm Up

1) a) star   b) triangle   c) pentagon
   d) star   e) heart

2) Number of figures with the same order: 3
   (the second, third and fifth figures all go from top to bottom in the order: square, trapezium, triangle).

Find the Figure Like the First Three

3) E
In all figures the semicircle must overlap one of the star's points.

4) A
In all figures there must be a four-sided shape on the left hand side of the figure. The circle must be on the right hand side of the figure.

5) C
In all figures the circles must go from left to right in the order: white, black, black, grey. (The order of the circles is always the same if you start from wherever the white circle is and move right. When the order reaches the right hand circle, it starts again from the left hand circle.)

Complete the Pair

6) D
The black segment moves round three places.

7) C
The line and the black dot swap places. The short grey triangle swaps places with the tall grey triangle.

8) D
All of the shapes move one place to the left. (When a shape reaches the far left, it starts again from the far right.)

Page 10 — Rotation

Warm Up

1) a) C   b) A   c) A   d) C   e) C   f) A

2) Number of identical figures: 2
   (the first and second figures).

Complete the Series

3) B
The arrows rotate 45 degrees clockwise in each series square. The number of arrows alternates between one and three.

4) E
The whole figure apart from the black triangle rotates 90 degrees anticlockwise in each series square. The black triangle rotates 180 degrees in each series square.

Page 11 — Reflection

Warm Up

1) a) yes   b) no   c) yes   d) no   e) no   f) yes

2) Number of reflections: 3
   (the first, third and fifth figures).

Complete the Pair

3) B
The figure reflects across.

4) C
The figure reflects downwards.

Pages 12-13 — Layering

Warm Up

1) a) circle   b) triangle   c) circle
   d) square   e) triangle   f) square

2) Number of ice creams: 4
   (the first, second, fourth and sixth ice creams all have a front scoop that is hatched, a middle scoop that is dotted and a back scoop that is grey).

Odd One Out

3) D
In all other figures, the black shape is at the front, and the white shape is at the back.

4) C
In all other figures, the crosshatched lemon is at the back and the dotted orange is at the front.

5) E
In all other figures, the black shapes are identical to the white shape made by the overlap of the two grey shapes.

Complete the Pair

6) A
The white inner shape made by the overlap of the other two shapes is cut out. The cut-out shape takes the shading of the first two shapes.

7) D
All of the overlapping lines disappear. The top shape moves to the back, and the bottom shape moves to the front.

8) A
The shape at the front of the top three shapes moves to the back.

Answers

Spatial Reasoning

Pages 14-15 — 3D Shapes

Warm Up

1) a) 2   b) 3   c) 3   d) 4   e) 5   f) 4

2) Number of figures which are different views of the figure in the square: 2 (the first option is the figure viewed from the back and the third option is the figure viewed from the right).

Look at the Figure from the Top

3) **D**
The figure should have two cubes at the front, which rules out options A, B and E. There are five cubes visible from above, which rules out option C.

4) **B**
There should be two cubes at the back of the figure, which rules out options A and E. There should be five cubes visible from above, which rules out options C and D.

5) **C**
There should be five cubes visible from above, which rules out options A, B and E. There should be a line of three cubes at the front of the figure, which rules out option D.

Look at the Figure from the Right

6) **E**
There should be a white block on the right-hand side of the figure, sticking out on its own at the front, which rules out options A, C and D. There should be a cube in the middle, which rules out option B.

7) **B**
There should be a white block two cubes long at the front of the figure, on the bottom, which rules out options A, C and E. This white block should stick out on the left-hand side, which rules out option D.

8) **D**
There should be a white cube on top of a grey block, which rules out options A and C. There should be a white block two cubes long at the front of the figure, which rules out options B and E.

Pages 16-17 — Folding

Warm Up

1) a) no   b) yes

2)

Fold Along the Line

3) **C**
Options A and B are ruled out because the fold line has moved. Option D has broken apart along the fold line. Option E is a rotation and hasn't been folded.

4) **D**
Options A and C are ruled out because the fold line has moved. Option B is ruled out because the part of the figure originally below the fold line is the wrong shape. Option E is ruled out because the part of the figure that has been folded is the wrong shape.

5) **B**
Option A is ruled out because the part of the shape originally to the right of the fold line should still be visible. Options C and E are ruled out because the part of the figure originally to the right of the fold line is the wrong shape. Option D is ruled out because the part of the figure that has been folded is the wrong shape.

Fold and Punch

6) **E**
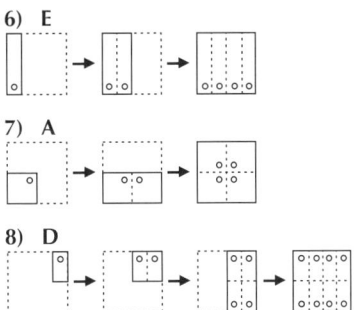

7) **A**

8) **D**

Page 18 — Hidden Shape

Warm Up

1) Shape b

2) a) 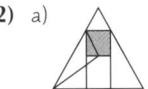   b)    c)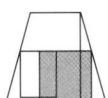

Hidden Shape

3) **E**

4) **D**

Page 19 — Connecting Shapes

Warm Up

1) Figure a

2) You could draw it in several ways. For example:

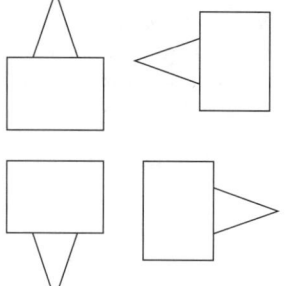

Connecting Shapes

3) **C**
Options A and E are ruled out because the triangle should be connected to the square. Option B is ruled out because the square is connected to the wrong side of the rectangle. Option D is ruled out because the wrong side of the triangle is connected to the square.

4) **A**
Options B, C and E are ruled out because the triangle and rectangle are connected to the wrong sides of the hexagon. Option D is ruled out because the wrong side of the rectangle is connected to the hexagon.

Pages 20-25 — Assessment Test 1

Section 1 — Odd One Out

1) **E**
In all other figures, the two small triangles are different colours.

2) **B**
In all other figures, half of the star's points are white.

3) **D**
In all other figures, the triangle at the bottom is on the left side of the line.

4) **A**
All other figures have two wavy lines and one straight line at the bottom.

5) **D**
All other figures are identical apart from rotation.

Section 2 — Complete the Pair

1) **C**
The figure reflects across.

2) **B**
One black dot is added to each half of the white circle.

3) **A**
The small shape turns black. It moves down and to the right so that it overlaps the edge of the large white shape.

4) **A**
The jagged line becomes wavy and the black dots turn white.

5) **C**
The figure rotates 90 degrees clockwise.

Section 3 — Complete the Grid

1) **B**
Working from left to right, an extra line appears around the white shape.

2) **A**
Working from left to right, the two figures (a black jagged shape and a white flag) alternate in each grid square.

3) **C**
Working from left to right, the jagged line moves up the white shape. The part of the shape below the jagged line is always black.

4) **A**
Working from left to right, the shading of the bottom left hand shape swaps with the shading of the top right hand shape.

Section 4 — Find the Figure Like the First Two

1) **A**
In all figures, the two outer stripes on the pencil must be the same colour and the inner stripe must be a different colour.

2) **B**
All figures must have two black ellipses at the bottom and five ellipses around the circle at the top.

3) **C**
All figures must have three shapes that are identical apart from size.

4) **E**
All figures must have a large white shape with a smaller, 180 degree rotation of the same shape inside it.

5) **D**
All figures must be divided in half with the bottom half shaded grey. They must all have three white circles.

Section 5 — Complete the Series

1) **C**
The series alternates between a grey orange with its stalk on the right, and a white pear with its stalk on the left.

2) **D**
One grey triangle is removed from the bottom of the figure in each series square.

3) B
Each shape moves clockwise around the four corners of the series square. The shading of the heart alternates between grey and white in each series square.

4) B
In each series square the three arrows rotate together 90 degrees anticlockwise. The gaps in the arrows get bigger in each series square.

5) A
A star is added in each series square. The colour of the stars alternates between white and black.

Section 6 — Vertical Code

1) B (X)
X = a grey hat band, Y = a black hat band.

2) D (LN)
K = flag on the right of the line, L = flag on the left of the line.
M = triangular flag, N = rectangular flag.

3) B (FQ)
F = three small rectangles, G = four small rectangles.
P = black rectangles, Q = white rectangles.

4) D (KS)
J = black and white stripes are on the left of the wavy shape,
K = black and white stripes are on the right of the wavy shape.
S = two thick black lines on the right, T = one thick black line.

Pages 26-31 — Assessment Test 2

Section 1 — Complete the Pair

1) D
The figure reflects across and the black shape turns white.

2) B
The small shape in the bottom left of the figure moves to the bottom right.

3) B
The inner shape gets bigger and moves to the back. The outer shape gets smaller and moves to the front.

4) A
The figure reflects downwards, gets smaller and turns grey.

5) E
One leaf and one circle are added to the figure.

Section 2 — Complete the Series

1) C
The triangle and the oval alternate in each series square.

2) A
The number of lines increases by one in each series square.

3) A
In each series square, the rocket rotates 45 degrees clockwise. The colour of the circle alternates between white and black.

4) B
In each series square, the circle moves down in the order: top, middle, bottom, top, middle. The black ellipse changes size in the order: small, medium-sized, big, small, medium-sized.

5) C
In each series square, the black shading moves up one shape.

Section 3 — Odd One Out

1) B
In all other figures, the line comes out of the side of the shape nearest to the set of three squares.

2) E
All other figures contain at least one white circle.

3) D
In all other figures, the small semicircle inside the large white shape has its flat side pointing down.

4) E
In all other figures, there are three short lines crossing the long line.

5) A
In all other figures, the two shapes overlap.

Section 4 — Vertical Code

1) B (L)
L = white circle, M = white triangle.

2) B (YW)
X = two hearts, Y = two squares.
W = the outline of the largest shape is solid,
Z = the outline of the largest shape is dashed.

3) A (BQ)
A = triangle, B = square, C = circle.
P = two black shapes, Q = one black shape.

4) E (ET)
E = spotted shape, F = crosshatched shape,
G = striped shape.
S = the bottom of the sock curves round to the left,
T = the bottom of the sock curves round to the right.

Section 5 — Complete the Grid

1) D
Working from left to right, the figure rotates 90 degrees clockwise.

2) A
Working from left to right, the shape reflects across.

3) A
Working from left to right, the shape moves diagonally up to the right. The shape's colour changes in the sequence: white, grey, black.

4) E
In the left hand grid square, both shapes are white. In the middle grid square, the left hand shape changes colour. In the right hand grid square, the right hand shape changes colour to match the left hand shape.

Section 6 — Find the Figure Like the First Three

1) A
All figures must have a white semicircle.

2) E
In all figures, there is a black square inside a white triangle.

3) D
All figures have two lines inside the large white shape.

4) D
All figures have a small shaded semicircle which is rotated the same way as the large semicircle.

5) B
If all figures are rotated so the small shapes are at the top, the shapes go from left to right in the order: star, heart, circle.

Pages 32-37 — Assessment Test 3

Section 1 — Find the Figure Like the First Two

1) B
All figures must be black curved arrows.

2) C
In all figures, both arrowheads point towards the curved lines.

3) D
All figures must have a black rectangle. The two ends of each semicircle must point towards the trapezium.

4) B
In all figures, the ribbons must be the same colour as the circle. The white star must have six points.

5) E
All figures contain two small black circles inside the large white shape and two white circles outside it.

Section 2 — Vertical Code

1) D (G)
F = the rocket has one fin, G = the rocket has two fins, H = the rocket has three fins.

2) B (JZ)
H = grey volcano, J = white volcano.
Y = two black drops, Z = three black drops.

3) E (AW)
A = black circles, B = black squares, C = black triangles.
V = black middle shape, W = white middle shape.

4) D (BY)
B = a small grey rectangle, C = a medium-sized grey rectangle, D = a large grey rectangle.
X = the outline of the outer rectangle is dashed, Y = the outline of the outer rectangle is solid.

Section 3 — Complete the Series

1) A
The flower gains a grey petal in each series square.

2) B
In each series square, a black shape appears in the next segment of the pentagon, going in a clockwise direction. The lines inside the pentagon alternate between dashed and solid.

3) A
In each series square, the hatched circle alternates between being behind and in front of the black six-pointed star.

4) E
The heart rotates 90 degrees clockwise in each series square and moves clockwise around the four corners of the series square.

5) A
All the dots move one place to the right in each series square. When they reach the right hand side, they start again from the left.

Section 4 — Complete the Grid

1) A
Working from top to bottom, the black shading turns grey.

2) B
Working from left to right, the colour of the large triangles changes from black to grey and the small inner triangle rotates 180 degrees.

3) B
Working from left to right, the line extends along one more side of the grid square.

4) C
Working from left to right, the figure rotates 45 degrees clockwise in each grid square.

Section 5 — Complete the Pair

1) A
The colours of the two shapes at the top of the figure swap over and the whole figure rotates 180 degrees.

2) A
The figure divides in half. The left half becomes dotted and the outline of the right half becomes dashed.

3) E
The figure rotates 180 degrees and two small white rectangles are added inside the white square.

4) B
The two arrows rotate together 90 degrees clockwise.

5) B
The top shape moves to the left and an identical shape appears on the right. The two lines rotate to join each top shape to the bottom shape.

Section 6 — Odd One Out

1) E
All other figures have a rainbow with three stripes.

2) E
In all other figures, the arrow is pointing towards the square.

3) A
When all figures are rotated so the coloured stripe is at the bottom, the square is on the right hand side in all other figures.

4) D
In all other figures, the cherry on the left is higher than the cherry on the right.

5) B
All other figures have five sides.

Pages 38-43 — Assessment Test 4

Section 1 — Complete the Series

1) C
The number of horizontal lines increases by one in each series square.

2) C
The shading in the left half of the shield moves to the right half of the shield in the next series square. A new type of shading appears in the left half.

3) B
The arrow and the circle rotate together 90 degrees clockwise in each series square. The colour of the circle alternates between white and black.

4) C
In each series square, one book is taken away from the right hand side of the figure.

5) D
The black and grey colours move up one shape in each series square. (When a colour reaches the top shape, it starts again in the bottom shape.)

Section 2 — Complete the Grid

1) E
Working from left to right, the hatching of the shape rotates 90 degrees (but the shape stays the same).

2) B
Working from left to right, the figure rotates 90 degrees clockwise, and the two shapes swap colours.

3) C
Working from left to right, the colour of the two circles changes from white, to grey, to black. The number of short lines at the top of the figure increases by one in each grid square.

4) B
Working from left to right, the figure reflects across and gets smaller.

Section 3 — Find the Figure Like the First Three

1) D
In all figures, the white shape must be on the end of the short line, and the black shape must be on the end of the long line.

2) C
All figures must have two white triangles.

3) E
All figures must have an arrow pointing to a black dot. The white circle must have one dot at the top, one at the bottom, one on the left and one on the right.

4) D
All figures must have an L-shaped line with a raindrop shape attached to the end of its shortest side. There must be three short lines coming out of the raindrop shape.

5) D
All figures must have two dashed lines coming down from the top of the curved shape. The dashed lines must be attached to a four-sided shape.

Section 4 — Odd One Out

1) B
In all other figures, the hatched shape is at the back.

2) A
All other figures have six sides.

3) C
In all other figures, the smallest smoke cloud is directly above the black semicircle.

4) C
In all other figures, the top two hearts are 180 degree rotations of the bottom two hearts.

5) A
In all other figures, the small shape is the same as the top half of the large shape, only smaller and a different colour. (In A, the shape is the same as a quarter of the large shape.)

Section 5 — Vertical Code

1) A (W)
W = four-sided shape, X = three-sided shape,
Z = five-sided shape.

2) C (BY)
A = circles, B = stars.
X = shapes on the left, Y = shapes on the right.

3) D (AV)
A = the point of the heart is at the bottom,
B = the point of the heart is on the right,
C = the point of the heart is at the top.
V = the heart has a solid outline,
W = the heart has a dashed outline.

4) B (CG)
A = grey wheels, B = white wheels, C = black wheels.
F = circular window, G = square window.

Section 6 — Complete the Pair

1) **A**
The figure gets larger and its shading changes to white spots on a black background.

2) **B**
The centre shape becomes larger and surrounds the other shapes. It swaps shading with the other small shapes.

3) **C**
The figure reflects across and turns grey.

4) **A**
The figure rotates 90 degrees clockwise and one circle is taken away.

5) **E**
The figure rotates 180 degrees and changes shading. A larger white version of the same shape appears behind it.

Pages 44-49 — Assessment Test 5

Section 1 — Complete the Pair

1) **D**
The figure rotates 180 degrees and the circles turn grey.

2) **A**
The lines move outside the large shape and the large shape disappears. The small white shape moves down.

3) **B**
The figure reflects across and the top shape turns black.

4) **B**
The white parts of the figure turn black and the hatched parts turn white.

5) **E**
The grey shapes move to the top of the white shape. The two black dots move to the bottom of the figure, outside the white shape.

Section 2 — Odd One Out

1) **B**
In all other figures, the straight line between the two shapes is dashed.

2) **E**
All other figures have six long lines that join in the middle.

3) **D**
All other figures are identical apart from rotation. (D is a reflection.)

4) **B**
In all other figures, the spiral goes in an anticlockwise direction (if you work from the centre outwards).

5) **E**
In all other figures, the two black shapes are on the same side of the line as each other (and the two white shapes are on the same side as each other).

Section 3 — Vertical Code

1) **C (BX)**
A = pointed vertical shapes, B = rounded vertical shapes.
X = black vertical shapes and white horizontal rectangle,
Y = white vertical shapes and black horizontal rectangle.

2) **E (GL)**
G = arrow pointing to the right, H = arrow pointing to the left.
K = one V-shaped line,
L = two V-shaped lines.

3) **B (EM)**
C = grey circle, D = white circle, E = black circle.
M = clockwise spiral (starting from the centre),
N = anticlockwise spiral.

4) **B (YC)**
W = one star, X = two stars, Y = three stars.
C = grey moon shape, D = white moon shape.

Section 4 — Complete the Grid

1) **E**
Working from left to right, the figure reflects across.

2) **B**
Working from left to right, the left hand shape moves above the right hand shape. The line joining the shapes rotates 90 degrees and another line is added.

3) **A**
Working from left to right, the figure rotates 90 degrees clockwise. The colour of the figure changes from white, to grey, to black.

4) **C**
In each row, the figure in the right hand grid square is made by joining the figure in the left hand grid square with the figure in the middle grid square. This new shape turns white.

Section 5 — Find the Figure Like the First Two

1) **A**
All figures must have four sides.

2) **A**
All figures must have a large square with one of its flat sides at the bottom. They must have two small grey triangles in two of the square's corners. Only two of each triangle's corners must touch the sides of the square (they point towards the middle of the square).

3) **D**
All figures must have a black ellipse and a white circle. The flag in each figure must point to the right.

4) **C**
All figures must be identical apart from rotation.

5) **C**
All figures must have a shape with one curved side and one flat side. The flat side must be at the bottom. This shape must be divided into four stripes, with a circle at the top.

Answers

Section 6 — Complete the Series

1) B
In each series square the line moves inside the egg shape in the order: bottom, middle, top, bottom, middle.

2) C
The figure rotates 90 degrees clockwise in each series square.

3) A
One dot is removed in each series square. The black shading inside the circle increases by one third in each series square. (When the circle is completely shaded, the pattern begins again with the first third shaded.)

4) A
In each series square, the black shape turns grey and the next shape on the right turns black.

5) D
In each series square, the black shape disappears and the shape above it turns black.

Pages 50-55 — Assessment Test 6

Section 1 — Find the Figure Like the First Three

1) B
All teacups must have one handle. If all the cups are rotated so the saucer is at the bottom, the handle must be on the right hand side.

2) A
All figures must have circles in front of each corner of the shape.

3) E
In all figures, the stalk must curve to the right and the flower must have four petals. Three petals must have the same shading, and the fourth must have a different shading.

4) E
All figures must have a knife, a fork and a spoon. If all the figures are rotated so the spoon is at the top, the knife must be on the left and the fork must be on the right.

5) D
All figures must have one grey shape and one white shape.

Section 2 — Complete the Series

1) C
Each star loses a point in each series square. The colour of each star alternates between grey and white.

2) C
The black shading moves one place towards the middle of the figure in each series square. (When the shading reaches the middle of the figure, it starts again from the outside.)

3) E
In this series, the number of sides of the shapes changes in the sequence: three, four, five, four, three. The outer shape must always be white and the inner shape must always be black.

4) A
An extra triangle is added in each series square. The colour of each triangle alternates between white and black.

5) A
The shaded part of the cupcake wrapper moves one place to the right in each series square. The colour of the cherry alternates between grey and black.

Section 3 — Odd One Out

1) B
If all the figures are rotated so the sheep is upright, the sheep's head is on the left in all other figures.

2) D
All other figures are hatched horizontally. (D is hatched vertically.)

3) D
All other figures have five white triangles.

4) A
In all other figures, the dashed line is next to a white section of the circle.

5) D
If the figures are rotated so the curved line coming out of the figure is at the bottom, the line curves to the left in all other figures.

Section 4 — Complete the Pair

1) C
The shape moves down and another identical shape appears above it. They both become hatched.

2) E
The long white shapes get shorter, and the short white shapes get longer.

3) B
The figure reflects across and the grey shapes turn white.

4) E
The large shape gets bigger and the small shapes move inside it. The large shape swaps colours with the two small shapes.

5) C
The figure rotates 90 degrees clockwise.

Section 5 — Complete the Grid

1) A
Working from left to right, the star turns grey and gains a point.

2) E
Working from left to right, the figure reflects across and becomes white with black dots.

3) D
In each row, the figure in the right hand grid square is made from the lines in the left hand square and the flower from the middle grid square.

4) B
Working from left to right, the figure rotates 90 degrees clockwise and gains one dot.

Answers

Section 6 — Vertical Code

1) **A (CN)**
C̲ = black centre, D = white centre.
M = circle, N̲ = square.

2) **C (SA)**
R = star on top of triangle, S̲ = circle on top of triangle.
A̲ = the shape leans to the left, B = the shape leans to the right.

3) **C (LQ)**
L̲ = both lines dashed, M = one line dashed and one line solid,
N = both lines solid.
P = lines on the left of the rectangle, Q̲ = lines on the right.

4) **E (YF)**
X = black outline, Y̲ = white outline.
E = four lines, F̲ = five lines, G = six lines.

Pages 56-61 — Assessment Test 7

Section 1 — Odd One Out

1) **A**
All other arrows have a solid line.

2) **E**
In all other figures, the black star has five points.

3) **C**
In all other figures, the shapes go from left to right
in the order: raindrop, star, pentagon.

4) **D**
In all other figures, the cactus has one big arm
and one small arm. (In D it has two big arms.)

5) **D**
All other figures have only one curved side.
(D has two curved sides.)

Section 2 — Complete the Grid

1) **A**
Working from left to right, the small shape moves up
diagonally to the opposite corner of the grid square.
A large black version of the same shape appears behind it.

2) **E**
Working from left to right, the figure reflects
across. The white shape gets smaller.

3) **D**
Working from left to right, one quarter of the original shape disappears
in each grid square and its colour changes from white, to grey, to black.

4) **B**
Working from left to right, the small shape at the
top changes from a star, to a circle, to a square.
A coloured stripe is added in each grid square.

Section 3 — Complete the Pair

1) **A**
The figure reflects across and colours of the shapes swap.

2) **B**
The circle gains an extra line. The colour of the
circle swaps with the colour of the lines.

3) **C**
The figure is reflected across and the
oval at the bottom gets bigger.

4) **B**
The shape at the front moves to the back.

5) **E**
The lines below the shape move up into the shape.
The figure rotates 45 degrees clockwise.

Section 4 — Vertical Code

1) **C (AY)**
A̲ = semicircle at the top and circle inside,
B = rectangle at the top and square inside.
X = black small shape, Y̲ = white small shape.

2) **B (FQ)**
F̲ = circle at the back, G = circle at the front.
P = black square, Q̲ = crosshatched square.

3) **E (ZT)**
X = wavy line, Y = jagged line, Z̲ = straight line.
S = black part of shape on left, T̲ = black part of shape on right.

4) **D (WD)**
V = sun at the back, W̲ = sun at the front.
C = one raindrop, D̲ = two raindrops, E = three raindrops.

Section 5 — Complete the Series

1) **B**
An extra triangle is added on the right in each series square.

2) **D**
The bird's position inside the series square changes
in the order: top, middle, bottom, middle, top.

3) **C**
In each series square, the grey circle moves two
places clockwise around the pentagon.

4) **C**
In each series square, the figure reflects across.
The white ellipse turns black and a new white ellipse appears.

5) **C**
The figure rotates 90 degrees clockwise in each series square.

Answers

Section 6 — Find the Figure Like the First Two

1) **D**
All figures must have one thick jagged line made up of four shorter lines inside an ellipse.

2) **C**
All figures must have three grey shapes and one white shape.

3) **D**
In all figures there must be a white line at the front, going diagonally down to the right.

4) **A**
All figures must have a four-sided shape at the top.

5) **E**
All figures must have three rings. Two must be the same colour and one must be different. The grey rings must be in front of the black rings.

Pages 62-67 — Assessment Test 8

Section 1 — Complete the Pair

1) **D**
The small shapes become crosshatched. The row of small shapes swaps places with the straight line.

2) **C**
The shapes move down and they swap colours.

3) **A**
The figure (except the black and white shading inside the small shape) reflects across. The shading stays the same.

4) **C**
The figure reflects across and the colour of the outer shape swaps with the colour of the inner shapes.

5) **B**
The outline of the large shape becomes dashed and the sails move to the back.

Section 2 — Vertical Code

1) **A (BG)**
B = four white petals, C = three white petals.
F = heart-shaped petals, G = raindrop-shaped petals.

2) **C (XQ)**
X = black triangles, Y = grey triangles, Z = white triangles.
P = the angle between the arrows is 90 degrees,
Q = the angle between the arrows is 45 degrees.

3) **B (MS)**
L = two small circles, M = one small circle,
N = three small circles.
R = large circle on the left, S = large circle on the right.

4) **D (PS)**
P = the small black shape is on the right,
R = the small black shape is on the left.
S = the wavy line is at the bottom of the shape,
T = the wavy line is at the top of the shape.

Section 3 — Complete the Series

1) **C**
The number of shapes changes in the order: one, two, three, two, one.

2) **A**
The shape rotates 90 degrees anticlockwise around the four corners of the series square. If the figure is rotated so its points are at the top, the black shading moves one place to the right in each series square.

3) **B**
The shapes move one place anticlockwise around the corners of the triangle in each series square.

4) **D**
The number of small black dots increases by one in each series square. The colour of the telephone alternates between white and grey.

5) **D**
In each series square, a circle is added, alternating between dashed and solid. The colour of the star in the middle of the figure alternates between white and black.

Section 4 — Complete the Grid

1) **D**
Working from left to right, the white shape takes the shading of the large shape. The large shape turns white. The dashed and solid outlines swap over.

2) **E**
Working from left to right, the whole figure reflects across. Grey shapes turn white and white shapes turn grey.

3) **A**
Working from left to right, one more black shape moves behind the white shape in each grid square.

4) **B**
Working from left to right, the cross rotates 45 degrees clockwise and the shapes move to stay in the same part of the cross. One extra shape turns black in each grid square.

Section 5 — Find the Figure Like the First Three

1) **D**
In all figures, there must be a wavy line inside both semicircles. The parts of the semicircles that touch in the middle must be different colours.

2) **A**
All figures must be identical apart from rotation. (The square must always be at the front and the triangle at the back.)

3) **C**
All figures must have two flame shapes coming out of the largest shape that are both the same colour.

4) **B**
All figures must contain a three-sided shape and a four-sided shape which overlap.

5) **A**
In all figures, each side of the arrow is crossed by a short line.

Section 6 — Odd One Out

1) **C**
In all other figures, the triangle is on the right of the rectangle.

2) **A**
In all other figures, the bows are bigger the further they are from the grey shape.

3) **D**
In all other figures, there are four small black squares.

4) **E**
In all other figures, the spirals go anticlockwise (if you work from the centre outwards).

5) **E**
All other figures have three small circles.

Pages 68-73 — Assessment Test 9

Section 1 — Find the Figure Like the First Two

1) **D**
All figures must have a large pentagon.

2) **D**
All figures must have two black triangles at the top. The grey shapes on the left and right of the figure must have four sides.

3) **A**
All figures are identical apart from rotation. (E is a reflection.)

4) **B**
All figures must have three shapes that are identical apart from size, and an arrow that points to the largest shape.

5) **B**
All figures must have two feathers that are identical apart from size. The smaller feather must be in front of the larger feather.

Section 2 — Odd One Out

1) **E**
In all other figures, the overlap of the two shapes is black.

2) **A**
In all other figures, the spiral goes anticlockwise (if you work from the centre outwards).

3) **E**
All other figures are divided into three sections.

4) **C**
In all other figures, the feet are reflections of each other. (In C, they are identical.)

5) **C**
In all other figures, the diagonal rectangle at the bottom is on the same side of the figure as the highest half of the top rectangle.

Section 3 — Complete the Series

1) **B**
The shading of the semicircle alternates between crosshatched and black. The position of the heart alternates between the left hand side and the right hand side of the series square.

2) **B**
In this series the rectangle moves clockwise around the four sides of the series square. The star gains a point in each series square.

3) **D**
In each series square, the white circles change size in the order: small, medium, large, medium, small.

4) **D**
In each series square, the white square loses a dot. The figure reflects across in each series square (the position of the white square alternates between the left and the right of the series square).

5) **A**
In each series square, the circle becomes more complete. The number of triangles at the top changes in the sequence: one, two, three, one, two.

Section 4 — Complete the Pair

1) **C**
The hatching inside the large shape rotates 90 degrees.

2) **A**
The triangle reflects across. The shape inside the triangle swaps places with the shape on top of the triangle.

3) **E**
The two shapes at the bottom move up to the top of the large black shape. The black shape at the top gets bigger.

4) **B**
The figure rotates 45 degrees anticlockwise and the smaller white shape turns black.

5) **E**
All the shapes move up one place and the top shape moves to the bottom. (Each shape keeps the same shading.)

Answers

Section 5 — Vertical Code

1) B (FP)
F = the wings are ellipses, G = the wings are semicircles.
P = white trapezium, Q = black trapezium.

2) E (JY)
J = thin arrow, K = thick arrow, L = medium arrow.
X = five-pointed star, Y = four-pointed star.

3) A (TN)
S = white jagged shape, T = black jagged shape,
U = grey jagged shape.
M = jagged shape at the front, N = jagged shape at the back.

4) D (VH)
V = grey semicircle on left, W = grey semicircle on right.
F = two small circles, G = two small squares,
H = two small triangles.

Section 6 — Complete the Grid

1) C
Working from left to right, the arrows each rotate 180 degrees. A small black version of the large white shape appears in the middle of the figure.

2) E
Working from top to bottom, the figure reflects across.

3) D
Working from top to bottom, the figure rotates 90 degrees clockwise. The number of shapes increases by one in each grid square.

4) B
Each figure (white star, black triangle and hatched square) only appears once in each row and column.

Pages 74-79 — Assessment Test 10

Section 1 — Complete the Series

1) A
In each series square, the white rectangle gets longer and the colour of the triangle alternates between white and grey.

2) A
The figure rotates 90 degrees clockwise in each series square. The wavy white shape alternates between being behind and being in front of the tree shape.

3) B
The number of shapes on the corners of the triangle changes in the sequence: one, two, three, one, two. The colour of the small inner circles alternates between grey and white.

4) D
In each series square, the figure rotates 90 degrees clockwise. The height of the clock alternates between tall and short.

5) B
Each shape moves up one place in each series square. When they reach the top, they start again at the bottom.

Section 2 — Complete the Grid

1) E
Working from left to right, the figure rotates 45 degrees clockwise, and the two circles swap places.

2) E
Working from left to right, the white shape reflects across and takes the same shading as the large shape on the left.

3) D
Working from left to right, an extra shape is added behind the central shape. This new shape is identical to it, only larger. In the second grid square the new shape is white and in the third grid square it is black. The black triangle in the corner rotates clockwise around the four corners of the grid square.

4) D
Each figure (short black pencil, medium white pencil and long grey pencil) only appears once in each row and column.

Section 3 — Vertical Code

1) A (QW)
P = small shape is a 180 degree rotation of the large shape,
Q = small shape has the same rotation as the large shape.
W = arrow shapes, X = heart shapes.

2) B (KT)
J = large grey shapes, K = large white shapes.
R = small rectangle, S = small pentagon, T = small hexagon.

3) C (CL)
C = three white circles, D = two white circles.
K = circles inside black shape, L = circles outside black shape.

4) B (AR)
A = solid outline, B = dashed outline.
R = one quarter grey, S = two quarters, T = three quarters.

Section 4 — Find the Figure Like the First Three

1) B
All figures must have two shapes. The dashed line must split the figure exactly in half (it must be a line of symmetry).

2) E
In all figures, the large shape must be three quarters of a circle. The two circles at the bottom must be grey.

3) B
In all figures, the wavy line must cross itself once.

4) D
All figures must have a dashed line joining two stars that are the same colour. The third star must be a different colour.

5) C
All figures must have a large white shape and at least one small black shape. All black shapes must overlap the edges of the white shape.

Answers

Section 5 — Odd One Out

1) E
All other figures have two four-sided shapes.

2) C
In all other figures, the flat ends of the bow tie shapes point towards the curved sides of the outer shape. (In C, the flat ends point towards the flat sides of the outer shape.)

3) B
In all other figures, the white line points to the left.

4) C
In all other figures, the two halves of the hearts closest to each other are the same colour.

5) A
In all other figures, both shapes at the bottom of the figure are in front of the white rectangle.

Section 6 — Complete the Pair

1) B
The figure rotates 90 degrees clockwise and is hatched going diagonally down to the right.

2) C
The figure gets smaller and rotates 90 degrees clockwise. All black shapes turn white and all white shapes turn black.

3) A
The outline of the large dotted shape becomes a solid arrow. The small white shape turns black.

4) D
The hatched segment moves one place clockwise and the grey segment moves one place anticlockwise.

5) B
The small shape moves down so that its top edge touches the bottom edge of the large shape. The line moves to the top of the figure.

Pages 80-85 — Assessment Test 11

Section 1 — Hidden Shape

1) E

2) B

3) C
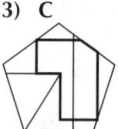

4) E

5) D
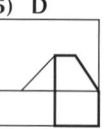

Section 2 — Look at the Figure from the Right

1) A
There should be a grey block in the middle of the figure, at the back. This rules out options B, C, D and E.

2) C
There should be a white cube on the left-hand side of the figure, at the front, which rules out options A, B, D and E.

3) A
There should be a white cube at the top of the figure, in the middle, which rules out options B, C and D. There should be a white cube at the bottom of the figure, at the back, which rules out option E.

4) E
There should be a white cube at the front of the figure, on the left, which rules out options A, B and C. There should be a white block, two cubes long, lying on its side at the top of the figure. This rules out option D.

Section 3 — Fold Along the Line

1) C
Options A, B and D are ruled out because the fold line has moved. Option E is ruled out because the figure has been broken apart along the fold line.

2) D
Options A and E are ruled out because the fold line has moved. Option B is ruled out because the part of the figure originally to the right of the fold line should still be visible. Option C is ruled out because the part of the figure originally to the right of the fold line is the wrong shape.

3) B
Option A is ruled out because the part of the figure that has been folded is the wrong shape. Option C is ruled out because the fold line has moved. Option D is ruled out because the part of the figure originally below the fold line should still be visible. Option E is ruled out because the figure has been broken apart along the fold line.

Answers

4) C

Option A is ruled out because the fold line has moved. Option B is ruled out because the figure has been broken apart along the fold line. Option D is ruled out because the part of the figure originally below the fold line is the wrong shape. Option E is ruled out because the part of the figure originally below the fold line should still be visible.

5) A

Option B is ruled out because the part of the figure that has been folded is the wrong shape. Options C and E are ruled out because the fold line has moved. Option D is ruled out because the part of the figure originally to the right of the fold line is the wrong shape.

Section 4 — Look at the Figure from the Top

1) C

There should be five blocks visible from above, which rules out options A, D and E. The cube sticking out of the right-hand side should be at the back of the figure, which rules out option B.

2) B

There should be five blocks visible from above, which rules out options A, C, D and E.

3) A

There should be five blocks visible from above, which rules out options B and C. There should be a line of four cubes going from right to left, which rules out options D and E.

4) A

There should be six blocks visible from above, which rules out options B and E. There should be a line of three cubes at the back of the figure, which rules out option C. There should only be one block at the front of the figure, which rules out option D.

Section 5 — Connecting Shapes

1) B

Options A, C and E are ruled out because the triangle should be connected to the rectangle. Option D is ruled out because the triangle is connected to the wrong side of the rectangle.

2) B

Options A and D are ruled out because the pentagon and the triangle are connected to the wrong sides of the trapezium. Option C is ruled out because the wrong side of the pentagon is connected to the trapezium. Option E is ruled out because the pentagon is connected to the wrong side of the trapezium.

3) C

Option A is ruled out because the triangle is connected to the wrong side of the pentagon. Options B and E are ruled out because the wrong side of the triangle is connected to the pentagon. Option D is ruled out because the square is connected to the wrong side of the pentagon.

4) E

Option A is ruled out because the wrong side of the L-shape is connected to the parallelogram. Option B is ruled out because the L-shape should not be connected to the rectangle. Option C is ruled out because the L-shape is connected to the wrong side of the parallelogram. Option D is ruled out because the L-shape and the rectangle are connected to the wrong sides of the parallelogram.

5) A

Options B and E are ruled out because the wrong side of the triangle is connected to the L-shape. Option C is ruled out because the wrong side of the parallelogram is connected to the L-shape. Option D is ruled out because the triangle and the parallelogram are connected to the wrong sides of the L-shape.

Section 6 — Fold and Punch

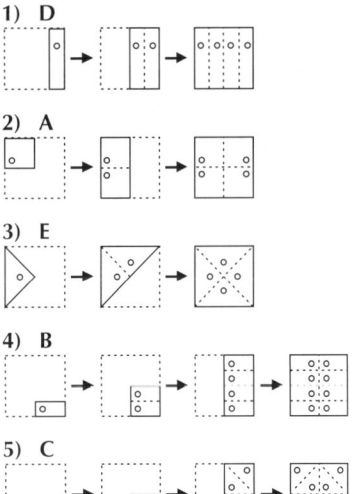

1) D

2) A

3) E

4) B

5) C

Answers

Progress Chart

Answer Sheets

Use this chart to keep track of your scores for the Assessment Tests.

You can do each test more than once — download extra answer sheets from cgpbooks.co.uk/11plus/answer-sheets or scan the QR code on the right.

Test	First Go		Second Go		Third Go	
	Date:	Score:	Date:	Score:	Date:	Score:
1						
2						
3						
4						
5						
6						
7						
8						
9						
10						
11						

Look back at your scores once you've done all the Assessment Tests. Each test is out of 28 marks. Work out which kind of mark you scored most often:

0-16 marks — Go back to basics and work on your question technique.

17-23 marks — You're nearly there — go back over the questions you found tricky.

24-28 marks — You're a Non-Verbal Reasoning star. Go on to Practice Book Ages 9-10.